"*God, I Need Help* brought healing to places I didn't even know needed healing. It helped guide me through some of my issues that have been compiling since the tornado and my mom's diagnosis of cancer."
*Kim, tornado survivor*

"A faith story like yours should be told! I came away with a deeper faith in God, trusting that He will provide no matter what the circumstance."
*Millissa, in job transition*

"My hope in God has been restored."
*Glenda, single mom*

"You have shown me what it is like to walk with Jesus! Total dependence on God leads to blessings in day-to-day living—the biggest blessing is a personal relationship with Christ."
*Jan, stay-at-home mom*

"Eye-opening! *God, I Need Help* convinced me I need to take everything to God."
*Nicole, childhood abuse survivor*

"Little details matter to God."
*Sylvia, multiple chemical sensitivities*

"I haven't had the same financial struggles, but I struggle with trusting God in other areas. The same principles apply to my fears. I need to run to God for refuge."
*Dee, home educator, three teenage sons*

"*God, I Need Help* shows the importance of an every-day relationship with God. Learn to rely on God before 'all else' fails."
*Deb, ongoing family health issues*

"I was challenged in how I pray. I have a renewed excitement and desire to be on my knees."
*Lisa, graduate student*

"When things get tough, where do you turn? *God, I Need Help* reinforced how powerful God can be in our life circumstances when we give everything to Him. No matter how bad things look, the Lord is there beside us to carry us through."
*Kim, mother of special-needs child*

"An amazing story of God's amazing faithfulness! It will be a blessing to all who read it."
*Louise, great-grandmother*

# *God, I Need Help*

### *A Woman in Distress Discovers God Is Absolutely Dependable*

by Linda Joyce Heaner

God loves you more than
you can imagine!

*Linda Joyce Heaner*

Jeremiah 31:3

# GOD I NEED HELP

## A WOMAN IN DISTRESS DISCOVERS
## GOD IS ABSOLUTELY DEPENDABLE

### Linda Joyce Heaner

*Essence* PUBLISHING

Belleville, Ontario, Canada

# God, I Need Help

Copyright © 2005  Linda Joyce Heaner

Unless otherwise noted, Scripture quotations are from *The Holy Bible, New International Version* © 1973, 1978, 1984 International Bible Society. Used by permission of Zondervan Bible Publishers. Scripture quotations marked NASB are from the *New American Standard Bible®* © 1960, 1977, 1995 by The Lockman Foundation. Used by permission. Scripture quotations marked CEV are from *The Holy Bible, Contemporary English Version* © 1995, American Bible Society.

**Library and Archives Canada Cataloguing in Publication**

Heaner, Linda Joyce, 1952-
        God, I need help : a woman in distress discovers God is absolutely dependable / Linda Joyce Heaner.
ISBN 1-55306-894-7.--ISBN 1-55306-896-3 (LSI ed.)

        1. Heaner, Linda Joyce, 1952-  2. Single mothers--Religious life.
3. Christian life.  4. Christian biography--United States.  I. Title.

BV4501.3.H42 2005        277.3'0085'2092        C2005-900616-1

**Quantity Discounts** are available. For more information, contact the address or Web site below:

Abiding Hope Ministries
P.O. Box 23506
Minneapolis, MN  55423-0506
www.abidinghope.com

*Essence Publishing* is a Christian Book Publisher dedicated to furthering the work of Christ through the written word. For more information, contact: 20 Hanna Court, Belleville, Ontario, Canada K8P 5J2.
Phone: 1-800-238-6376. Fax: (613) 962-3055.
E-mail: publishing@essencegroup.com
Internet: www.essencegroup.com

*To all who have wondered if God would
tire of hearing their prayers or meeting
their needs:*

*May God reveal His endless love and
faithfulness to you.*

# Table of Contents

# Acknowlegments

My heart overflows with gratitude to all who are named and unnamed below:

Lois, who first encouraged me and prayed with me about writing this story; Gretchen, Twyla, and Robbie— my initial editing and prayer team; all who prayed for me during the years of writing, revising, and seeking publication; those who gave me computers and instruction in using them; all who read the manuscript and gave me valuable feedback; the Thursday morning Women's Bible Study group at Hope Church for their encouragement, prayers, and willingness to "test" the book in a group setting; Rachel and Heidi, for their editing skills; Wes and Gretchen, and all who showed me God's faithfulness during these years; and my children, Timothy, Rachel, and Jonathan, who traveled this adventurous journey of trusting God with me and encouraged me to write this book.

Most of all I thank our Heavenly Father, for revealing Himself to me through difficult circumstances. I thank Him that I can share His faithfulness with others through this book. All glory goes to Him.

# Preface

Dear Reader,

When I face persistent struggles in my life, I am encouraged by stories from the lives of Christians like George Mueller, Amy Carmichael, and Hudson Taylor. They clung to God in the midst of relentless problems. Their circumstances differed from mine, yet their stories encourage me to trust God. Through their struggles, I see God more clearly. I witness His active involvement in their lives. Their stories give me hope to believe that the same God they trusted, who faithfully helped them, will also help me.

*God, I Need Help* is a compilation of stories of how God proved His faithfulness to me. It describes a tumultuous ten-year journey filled with both ordinary and severe distress. Gradually I discovered God's long-term commitment to care for my family and His limitless resources to meet our needs. God's unconditional love changed me.

Your life situation differs from mine. But all of us experience distress. All of us long for security and stability. So come with me on this journey from a place of fear and distress to a position of security and rest. Witness the compelling evidence of God's unending faithfulness!

I'm praying that as you read God will personally encourage you and you will become more aware of His faithfulness in your life.

*Linda Joyce Heaner*

*In my distress I called to the LORD; I cried to my God for help. From his temple he heard my voice; my cry came before him, into his ears (Psalm 18:6).*

## Chapter One

# God is My Provider

*For the eyes of the LORD move to and fro
throughout the earth that He may strongly
support those whose heart is completely His*
(2 Chronicles 16:9, NASB).

### Shattered

I hesitated outside the welfare office. College-educated, in my thirties, the mother of three children ages one, three, and six, I never expected to end up here. But I was desperate. Taking a deep breath, I stepped inside to apply for Aid to Families with Dependent Children (AFDC). *Oh God, help me through this.*

The clerk handed me a pile of paperwork. Every conceivable question about my family, education, work history, and finances required detailed answers. *Even close friends don't know all these things about me!* Not that the questions were wrong or that I had anything to hide, but my personal dignity and privacy were being stripped away. I felt like I was sitting there naked.

I filled out the endless forms in a large, bare room, then waited for more than an hour. At last I heard a male monotone voice call out "Linda Heaner." I hurried over to the drab, three-foot-wide cubicle. The young intake worker behind the desk took my application papers and scrutinized each answer.

"Do you have a savings account?" he questioned, his head buried in the paperwork.

"Yes, with less than thirty dollars in it."

"Do you have a checking account?"

"Yes."

"Any assets?"

*Is he going to repeat every single question in those forms?* "A '76 Ford station wagon with 120,000 miles, condemned by a mechanic as unsafe to drive." *If you call that an asset.*

The worker droned on through each question. *Doesn't he believe what I wrote? Oh God, please let us qualify for help.* I anxiously sat on the edge of my chair, awaiting his verdict.

Finally, for the first time, he looked directly at me for a few seconds. "*All* this information must be verified," he emphasized. "Sign these release forms so the county can obtain up-to-date facts from your bank and your landlord and also initiate child-support collection procedures. *If* everything here is accurate, you and your children will *probably* be eligible for AFDC."

I breathed a deep sigh of relief. *This humiliation is worth it if I can get help for my family.*

"*If* you qualify," the clerk continued, "the monthly grant for a family of four is $621. That amount would be prorated since it's already April 4. A check wouldn't be ready until the end of April, and you'd have to pick it up here. Future checks would be mailed by the first of each month."

"But it's almost four weeks until the end of the month! What help can I get *now*?"

"Have you received an eviction notice?"

"No."

"Have your utilities been turned off?"

"No."

"Then there's no emergency. There's nothing we can do for you."

*No emergency! What do you call this? My husband moved out two days ago, and I have three young children to care for.* "But I need help right now," I pleaded. "I only have a few dollars. I don't have a job. My children need food and diapers." I dug my fingernails into my palms, trying to hold back my tears.

"Once this information is verified, we determine what assistance you can receive. *We* notify *you*. There's nothing we can do for you right now," he repeated like a recording.

I felt the walls closing in on me. I couldn't breathe. *I'm not just a number in your computer or a case in your files. This is my life!* My vision blurred as I stumbled toward the door. The bright sunshine outside couldn't penetrate the bleak cloud descending over me. I sobbed uncontrollably as I drove home. *Why did I come here for help? How will I care for my children? What am I going to do?*

And so began my journey of learning to depend on God in ways I'd never had to before.

### Panicked

Growing up in a Christian family, as a young child I loved Jesus. As I studied the Bible in college, God revealed more of His personal love for me. I learned to trust God when I graduated and moved to a new city without a place to live. I searched for work in Christian education, and God provided positions in several churches. For years I taught and encouraged people of all ages to fully trust God.

Nearly ten years ago, I married a Christian man. As our family expanded, we welcomed our children as precious gifts from God. We weathered serious financial problems, including periods of unemployment. Our money problems skyrocketed when our youngest child was born and we had no medical insurance.

Those life experiences did not adequately prepare me for my present crisis. *Where are you, God? What's going to happen to my children and me? Will we end up out on the street? How can we live with no money? How will I pay for rent or utilities or food?*

Each day I met with God and poured out my heart to Him. *Help me, God. I don't know what to do. I've been home with my children since they were born. What do I do now? Please restore my marriage during this time of separation.*

God comforted me with promises from His Word, but worries and fears continued to deluge me. *Help me, God. I feel like I'm drowning.*

### Part of My Provision

How could I tell people my heart was breaking? This was not a topic for casual conversation. *Oh, hi. By the way, Mark and I are separated for six months while we reconcile our marriage.* I told a few friends at church. The news spread; the silence was deafening. People I'd known for years now seemed to avoid me. *Please don't shut me out. You don't know our financial crisis or ongoing employment struggles. We barely make ends meet. You don't know the arguments and hurtful words that have poisoned our home. This separation is*

*meant to restore our marriage. I'm doing everything I k
how to do. I want our marriage to work. Please help me—don't
condemn me.*

Memories of my experience at the welfare office tormented me: the silent condescension, the aloof interview, the absence of compassion. *How can I ever explain to anyone that I don't have any money and I applied for AFDC?* People I knew looked down on those receiving public assistance. I'd heard them talk about it in the past.

"They're lazy," one commented.

"They need to work instead of wasting our tax money."

"They're just looking for a handout," a third concluded.

*If people knew I applied for AFDC, they would think that way about me.* Suddenly I wanted to crawl into a hole and never come out. I didn't want anyone to know what I had done. Somehow applying for AFDC meant I was a failure.

One morning, while I was bemoaning my situation and crying out to God, He spoke to me. It wasn't an audible voice, but a thought that I knew wasn't my own entered my mind. "This welfare assistance is *part of My provision* for you at this time. Receive it that way." That phrase echoed through my mind. *Part of My provision...part of My provision...* Those words soothed my troubled heart. *God does care about what's happening in my life right now.*

*Part of My provision....God will use the welfare system to provide for some of our needs!*

*Part of My provision... not "all of My provision." God will also provide in other ways.*

*Part of My provision.... God will help me. I will not succumb to the "loser" mentality that can accompany welfare.* Instead of feeling ashamed that I had applied for public assistance, I began thanking God for how He would provide for us through it.

On April 12, a letter arrived from the county. "You are eligible to receive $621 per month from AFDC and $125 per month in food stamps. Medical Assistance will provide health insurance for your family. Your prorated check of $554 for April can be picked up on April 29, 1988." The county claimed total rights to any child-support payments I might receive during the time I received AFDC. However, every month child support was paid, I would receive a fifty dollar "bonus" check. *Thank You, Father. You are taking care of us.*

God reminded me of His promise: "For the eyes of the LORD move to and fro throughout the earth that He may strongly support those whose heart is completely His" (2 Chronicles 16:9, NASB).

### *The Other Part*

*It will be more than two weeks until I can pick up that check, God. How can I buy food or gas without any money? I can't instantly find a job after being home for six years. And day-care expenses for three children would be astronomical. Besides, this separation is meant to be temporary, just six months. So what do I do right now?*

The "other part" of God's provision began pouring in for our immediate needs. On hearing of our separation, an acquaintance drove to my home and gave me $100. Someone brought over three bags of clothes for my children. A relative mailed us $100.

Two weeks after separating, my estranged husband announced his decision to file for divorce. *What's going on? Why can't we work through our problems? God, this is not what You want or what I want. Oh God, please heal and restore our marriage.*

For seven months we had attended counseling together; now I continued alone. *I don't know how I'll pay for this, but I know I need help through this crisis.* The counselor graciously offered me a payment rate below the sliding-fee scale. *Thank You, Lord.*

I called Rent Assistance on May 1 to report changes in our family size and income. "My husband moved out," I said. "My children and I now receive AFDC."

"Your monthly rent payment is based on a percentage of your current income," the woman explained. "Starting in June, your portion of the rent will be reduced." *Our family qualified for this program last year. Now it makes it possible for my children and me to remain in this two-bedroom apartment. Lord, You are providing for us. I feel Your loving arms surrounding us.*

### A Workable Way

A woman from church called me. "Starting in June I'll need part-time child care for my two children in my home," Deb explained. "I thought you might be interested, Linda. You could bring your children along. It would be three days a week, early morning to mid-afternoon, throughout the summer."

"Thanks for asking me, Deb," I replied, after discussing more details. "I'll think it over and let you know in a day or two."

I called my caseworker immediately. "How would a job affect my AFDC grant?" I inquired.

"If you earn money, your grant is lowered."

"What?"

"It's hard to explain. A detailed formula figures it out."

"So if I earn money, I'm penalized?" I retorted, trying to control my anger.

"Well, yes, but if you earn less than $100 a month, your grant won't change. Besides, you're always better off than if you weren't working at all.

*"That's debatable. This system is crazy. Any steps I take to improve my financial position are sabotaged.* "What about doing day care for a friend?"

"That's still income. Any money from working that touches your hands must be reported as income within ten days." Then the worker paused. "You *can* barter," she said. "You baby-sit and that person buys you groceries or pays one of your bills. As long as no money touches your hands, bartering isn't counted as income."

"So if the person agrees to some form of bartering, it won't affect my grant?"

"That's right."

*My top priority right now is caring for my children. This job would enable me to do that. But would Deb be willing to barter? God, if You want me to take this job, please show us a way that's within the welfare rules yet not a burden for Deb.*

"I'd like to provide child care for you, Deb," I said, sitting at her kitchen table, "but there's one problem. In the welfare system, if I'm paid money directly for working, my grant is decreased. If I barter or receive the benefit of the money indirectly, it's not considered income and doesn't affect my grant. Could we barter somehow without making extra work for you?"

After discussing different options, Deb suggested a unique idea. "Here's what I'll do, Linda. I'll open a separate checking account and deposit in it the money I would pay you. Then I can write checks for expenses you have.

Will that work for you?"

*Will that work? Oh, Father, You are wonderfully creative in the ways You provide. Thank You for Deb.*

### Practical Help

"Linda, I've decided to find a safe, dependable car for you," Tom told me in May. This announcement from my brother-in-law surprised me.

"Really?" I replied. "I don't have much money to spare." Our car was not reliable. I worried about it breaking down every time I drove it. But compared to my marriage crisis, the car problem seemed minor.

Tom called again a few weeks later. "I'm still looking for a car for you," he said. "I haven't found a good one yet. I'm searching for a car my wife would feel comfortable driving our children around in."

*That's a nice thought, but it's not going to happen. Besides, I couldn't pay for a car if he found one.* I quickly forgot about Tom's car search. Other pressing issues consumed my thoughts.

My job at Deb's provided a welcome routine for our family three days a week. We played games with Deb's children in their spacious backyard. Nearly every day we walked to the neighborhood park. We enjoyed playing outdoors in the summer sun.

One July morning at Deb's the doorbell rang. When I opened the door, a man asked, "Are you Linda Heaner?"

"Yes," I replied.

"Please sign for this package," he said. Then he handed me a thick mailing envelope, walked to his car, and drove off. *That's strange. Why would anything be delivered to me here?*

I slowly opened the package, wondering what it contained. *Divorce papers! I can't believe this is happening. Oh God, I don't want a divorce.* As I read the papers, a crushing burden descended on me. I collapsed into a chair. *What am I going to do?* I tried to think clearly, but a deep fog clouded my mind. *My life is falling apart. I feel like I'm drowning in quicksand.* I sat there for a long time, paralyzed by fear. Tears streamed down my face. *I've got to pull myself together. I've got to make lunch for these five children running all over the house. But God, what's going to happen to me? How will I care for my children? Please help me.*

A few days later Tom called. "Linda, I've found a great car for you!" he exclaimed. "The engine is rebuilt. The body is in good shape. It's easy to drive and gets good mileage."

"Tom, I trust your judgment. If you think it's a good car, then it is. But I have no savings," I confessed, "no down payment, no credit. I don't think I could get a loan anywhere. I'm sorry you've done this whole car search for nothing."

Undaunted, Tom replied, "I'll make some phone calls and see what I can find out."

*You'll see; no one will give me a loan. Besides, I just got divorce papers. My whole life is falling apart. A different car isn't even in the picture.*

Tom called back the next day. "Linda, I've arranged a loan through my bank," he announced, "and I'll co-sign. Your payments will be less than $100 a month."

So I became the owner, sight unseen, of a '82 Chevy Citation. When we picked up the car, Tom said, "Linda, if you ever have trouble making a payment, call me and I'll cover for you, so you can get your credit rating built up."

My children and I received that car as God's special provision for us. *Thank You, God, for this dependable car. Thanks for Tom. Your timing is perfect! You not only provided the car, You're also providing the money for car payments through my child-care job at Deb's house. You are taking care of us.*

### Heart Care

"Hi, Linda," a cheery voice greeted me on the phone in August. "It's Carol."

"Carol!" I exclaimed. "It's so good to hear your voice. This connection is great. Where are you calling from?"

"We're only ten miles away," she laughed. "Jim is on study leave from our mission work in Japan. We'll be living here while he's in graduate school. What's going on with you?"

"Mark and I are separated. It was meant to last six months to reconcile our marriage, but he's filed for divorce," I quavered. "Things are pretty rough right now."

Carol and I had shared an apartment the year before I got married. We lost contact after she and her husband moved to Japan six years ago. Now we made plans to meet for an extended lunch. *Thank You, Lord, for sending Carol, a friend from the past who knows and loves me, someone I can talk to and pray with. Thank You for bringing her family here at this time.*

"I'm so glad you're here," I whispered as I hugged Carol the following week. Seeing her made my heart feel lighter than it had felt in months.

"Carol, before we go out to eat, will you help me pick out a television?" I asked. "I've shopped around but I can't decide on one. I thought you could advise me on the

Japanese models." Carol laughed and gladly agreed to help me.

Making any decisions at that time in my life was nearly impossible. Fears paralyzed my thinking. I had carefully saved money for a TV, but agonized over spending it. *What if our car breaks down? What if something bad happens to one of us? That money would be gone. Should I save it for emergencies? Is it wrong for me to buy a TV?* Even after convincing myself it was okay to buy a TV, I had returned home empty-handed twice.

I didn't share my mental anguish with Carol that morning. Instead, following her advice, I bought a standard, no-frills TV for our family. Afterwards, we lingered over lunch, catching up on the past six years.

Then Carol interrupted our pleasant conversation, gently urging, "Linda, tell me what's happening with you right now." Her personal invitation to share my pain opened a floodgate within me. Out flowed my hurt, anger, confusion, and fear. Carol's eyes conveyed tenderness as she listened intently. Both of us cried as I related the whole story. *Father, thank You for my dear friend. For the first time since the separation, I feel fully loved and accepted.*

"Linda," Carol said as we drove home, "Jim and I have money set aside in what we call 'The Lord's Fund.' We use it as He directs us. I feel strongly, and I'm sure Jim would agree, that God wants us to use that money to pay for your TV. I'll write out a check for that amount. Please receive it as a gift from God."

Tears streamed down my face. *God, You are so good. I finally trust You enough to spend my money on a TV, and now You provide this gift.*

God blessed our friendship in the following weeks and months. Carol and I grew closer than we had ever been, talking on the phone, sharing our hearts, and spending time together. Our children quickly became friends. They loved our weekly outings to parks and lakes. While they played together, we talked and prayed. *Father, thank You for Carol. I don't have to pretend with her but can share whatever I'm thinking or feeling. She is a precious gift sent by You to bring me comfort and hope in this difficult time.*

### Long-term Investments

A flyer for a correspondence writing course caught my attention. *I've always enjoyed writing. Maybe I could learn to write for magazines. But why am I even thinking about it? I could never save all the money needed for tuition.* Still, I kept the flyer and set aside twenty-five dollars.

Weeks later, in October 1988, an anonymous envelope containing $200 arrived in the mail. *This money can pay the remaining tuition I need to enroll in that writing course! Now I can pursue writing at home, while giving my children the loving attention they need.* I mailed my application and check that same day.

When the course materials arrived, I discovered that all my assignments had to be typed. *Oh no. I don't have a typewriter or the money to buy one. How will I ever get my papers typed? Why did I ever think I could do this? I'll probably have to withdraw from the course. I've failed before I've even started.*

A few days later, I received a card and a generous check from Bobbie and her husband, people from my church whom I'd never met. "We learned of your situation a while ago," they wrote. "We wanted to help but weren't able to until now." *Oh God, Your timing is amazing. You knew my need and provided this money right now. Thanks for Your clear encouragement to pursue this writing course.* I spent most of the money on a typewriter. Bobbie was delighted that their gift would help me develop my writing skills.

In January 1989, Bobbie called. "Linda, we'd like to give your daughter Rachel a scholarship to attend our church preschool next fall. It would bless her and give you some time each week for whatever you need to do."

I tried to respond, but no words would come. *Here I am, struggling to get through one day at a time, and people I barely know are thinking about our family's future. Father, You do have good plans for us!* I remembered God's promise: "For I know the plans I have for you," declares the LORD, "plans to prosper you and not to harm you, plans to give you hope and a future" (Jeremiah 29:11).

## A New Home

My three children and I constantly tripped over one another in our cramped, two-bedroom, second-floor apartment. *If only we had a little more space, daily living would be less stressful.*

Our family had qualified for a three-bedroom unit through Rent Assistance in 1987, but we couldn't find one then. Three-bedroom places were rare in our city. Some were not suited for families; others wouldn't accept Rent Assistance.

In February 1989 I began praying and searching for housing again. I registered with several low-income housing projects in the metro area. Some had two-year waiting lists. I searched for three months without any success. Depression became my daily companion. *There are no places available. I'm ready to give up. How can I even consider* *moving? Rent and utilities will increase at least $100 a month if I move, but my income will stay the same.*

Feeling absolutely desperate, I cried out to God once more. *Lord, I feel totally hopeless and helpless. These are our most basic needs: a three-bedroom place to live, with laundry facilities and a safe play area for my children. Please help me.*

Bobbie arrived at our apartment late one afternoon. "I got lost driving here," she explained, "but I discovered a three-bedroom duplex for rent only a few blocks away! Here's the address and the phone number from the rental sign."

I glanced at the address. "I looked at a duplex on that street two years ago. The three-bedroom unit was on the second floor. I'm sick of living on the second floor. Every time my children go outside or come in, I have to go downstairs and open the door for them. I can't handle living on the second floor anymore," I moaned.

"You could call and ask about it," Bobbie encouraged.

The following afternoon, I finally got up enough energy to make the phone call. "Hi," I said, "I'm calling about the three-bedroom duplex that's for rent."

"The one available is on the first floor," the owner replied, giving other details about the duplex.

I took a deep breath and began the awkward part of the conversation. "I'm a single mom with three children. I have a housing voucher. That means I pay a portion of the rent and Rent Assistance pays the rest. I qualify for a three-bedroom unit because I have two sons and a daughter. Are you familiar with Rent Assistance? Would you be willing to work with me in this program?"

"I've worked with Rent Assistance before," he replied kindly. "I'll be showing the house to someone at

4:00 p.m. But I'd be glad to show it to you at 3:30 pm."

"I'll be there!" I exclaimed. *It's already 3:00. There's no time to find someone to watch my children; they'll have to come with me. Now don't get excited. You've had your hopes up before, only to be disappointed. Can you believe it? A three-bedroom duplex on the first floor!*

With my children in hand, I quickly surveyed the house. *It has much more room than we have right now.* The basement had laundry hookups, lots of storage space, and a large area we could use as a playroom. *Could this be Your answer to my prayer, Lord? It has everything I asked You for: three bedrooms, a laundry area, and a big yard to play in. And it's on the first floor.*

I filled out the rental application apprehensively. *The rent here is $680. That's more than our monthly AFDC check. What portion would I pay? What will utilities cost here? Can I afford to move? Can I afford not to?*

Fear gripped me as I drove home. The paperwork would take five to seven days to process before we'd know if we could move there. Today was April 28. *I have to give my current landlord thirty days' notice if I want to move at the end of May. If I give notice but we're not accepted there, we'll have no place to live. If I move without giving thirty days' notice, I'll have to pay an extra month's rent, which I don't have. God, help me trust You. Please show me what to do.*

Seven-year-old Timothy and I talked more about the house at bedtime. "When would we move?" he asked.

"If everything is approved," I answered, "we would move at the end of May."

Timothy's eyes sparkled. "Mom," he whispered, "our new house would be like a big birthday present from God to you!" My birthday was May 30.

*It is remarkable how Bobbie drove by that house when she got lost. And the owner did show it to us right away. Could this be Your answer to my prayer, Lord?*

The next morning I gave notice to my current landlord. Fear pummeled me relentlessly. *What's going to happen to us? Was I foolish to give notice? Will we be able to move to the duplex? Help me, God.* After six terrifying days fighting panic and worry, we were approved to rent the duplex. *Thank You, Lord!*

Several days later, I called the owner of the duplex. "Will you please make sure all the carpets are thoroughly cleaned before we move in?" I asked timidly. "My two-year-old son crawls on the floor a lot, and the current renters have a dog."

"I'll do better than that," he replied. "I'm going to put in new carpeting, a new linoleum kitchen floor, and new wallpaper."

*Lord, Your provision of this new home is far beyond my wildest dreams. You are so good to us. Now I bring You all our needs in moving: boxes for packing, a washer and dryer, vehicles for moving, and people to help us.*

God provided generously. We borrowed a flatbed trailer and a van to transport our belongings. A friend cared for Rachel and Jonathan while Timothy and I helped move. Another friend unpacked all our kitchen boxes. Someone assembled the beds. Bobbie brought curtains and bookcases. When she learned we didn't have a washer or dryer, she said, "Go pick out the ones you want. You can repay me when you get back on your feet."

*Father, this is like moving into a brand new house: polished cabinets and woodwork; new wallpaper, carpeting, and kitchen floor; everything freshly painted; and something I hadn't noticed before—a fireplace. God, You are so good! You handpicked this house for us. It's the nicest home we've ever lived in.*

The location of our new home was ideal: two blocks from the baseball fields; three blocks from school; and four blocks from the park, skating rink, and library. We were one mile from the freeway, yet in a quiet neighborhood. We soon learned more about the uniqueness of our home: no other first-floor duplex nearby had a basement, a storage shed, or three bedrooms. *How great is Your love for us, God. Please give us many opportunities to tell others how You've blessed us with this home.*

\* \* \*

1. The word "support" means: to hold up; to serve as a foundation for; to keep from fainting, yielding or losing courage; to carry or comfort; to be an advocate. Which kind of support do you need right now? 2 Chronicles 16:9 (NASB) says, "For the eyes of the LORD move to and fro throughout the earth that He may strongly support those whose heart is completely His." How does this promise apply to you?

2. Share a situation when God provided exactly what you needed at just the right time. Do you regularly recognize God's provision for your family? Why or why not?

3. Describe a time when you felt hopeless or abandoned. What were your thoughts and feelings? What helped you get through it? How might you convey God's love to someone who is overwhelmed by difficult circumstances?

*Father, please open my eyes to see Your daily provision in my life.*

*Chapter Two*

# God Is Always With Me

*The LORD your God is the one who goes with
you. He will not fail you or forsake you*
(Deuteronomy 31:6, NASB).

### Abiding Hope

For nearly eighteen months I remained hopeful that
my marriage would be restored, my desire since our separation. *The legal papers state "irreconcilable differences."
That's not true. I know we can work things out. God will help
us.* Sadly, no reconciliation occurred. The chasm between
my estranged husband and me deepened. Yet I still
believed God would intervene. After all, God designed
marriage; ours was a Christian marriage; and nothing
was impossible for Him.

One afternoon in August 1989, the truth hit me like a
bombshell: I was going to court in a few weeks for a
divorce I couldn't prevent. *Where are You in all of this, God?
Why aren't You restoring our marriage? I committed it to You,*

*but it doesn't look like You're doing a thing. I thought if I kept praying and walking closely with You, You'd transform our marriage. Why don't You do something? You're the God who specializes in miracles. Why aren't You helping me?* I wept bitterly until I had no tears left.

Then a quiet voice spoke to my heart. I knew it was Jesus. "Linda, don't look at your husband. Don't look at people. Don't look at your circumstances. Look at Me. I am your Abiding Hope."

In the silence, words quickly came to my mind and I wrote them down. Soon a melody flowed from my heart and I wrote it down. I began singing the song. Fresh tears flowed freely because I knew this message was true. As I sang the words over and over again, God brought hope and healing to my heart.

*Abide in Me, Jesus said, and I'll abide in you*
*In Me there is fullness of life*
*Come rest in My embrace and daily seek My face*
*In Me alone you will find:*

*Abiding Hope, to guide you through the night*
*Abiding Hope, so in the darkness you'll see light*
*Abiding Hope, to keep you anchored through the storms*
*I'm here to be your Abiding Hope*

*He's changing me deep inside, and I'm still learning to abide*
*He's my joy, He's my fullness of life*
*My strength for each new test, my peace, my quiet rest*
*In Jesus alone I have found:*

*Abiding Hope, to guide me through the night*
*Abiding Hope, so in the darkness I'll see light*
*Abiding Hope, to keep me anchored through the storms*

*My Jesus is my Abiding Hope*
*My Jesus is and always will be my Abiding Hope*

That moment with Jesus changed me. *Jesus is the only One I can completely depend on. He will be my strength in the days ahead.* God reminded me of the numerous ways He had cared for our family during the past year and a half: a dependable car, daily necessities, a spacious home, countless people who cared for my children, gifts of money, and a variety of friends. *God, You have provided for all our needs!*

God gave me a powerful message to share with others. *In every situation, Jesus is our Hope. He is trustworthy and dependable. When we're overcome by the circumstances of life, we can cling to Him. He is our Abiding Hope.*

God began opening new doors for me. A publisher contacted me to write youth resource materials. *My training from that writing course will help me now. God does have plans for me to write!* I was invited to speak and sing at three different events, all scheduled the same week as the court hearing. With each group, I emphasized how Jesus is our Abiding Hope in every situation. I sang "Abiding Hope" at a women's luncheon, right before driving to the courthouse.

Through all these events, God said to me, "Linda, I have good plans for you in the future. I intend to use you to draw others closer to Me. I grieve with you over this divorce. I will continue to care for you and your children because I love you."

### Heartbroken

I was not emotionally prepared for the court hearing that day in September. I had met with my lawyer several times, but our conversations never involved heart issues. In court, the divorce proceedings were matter-of-fact, void of all emotion. *This is my life and my future we're talking about. My heart is being ripped out and torn into a million pieces. Doesn't anyone care? Thirty minutes before a judge, and my marriage is legally destroyed.* I maintained my composure in court, but grief engulfed me as I drove home alone that afternoon.

My children were happily playing at a friend's house, unaware of the events at the courthouse. When I arrived to take them home, seven-year-old Timothy shouted "Mommy, watch me!" as he proudly whizzed by on a bicycle. He had learned to ride a two-wheeler during the few hours I'd been gone. *We will remember this day for different reasons: joy and sadness, accomplishments and failures.*

That evening, I told Timothy and Rachel about the divorce.

"When did Daddy live with us?" they questioned.

"Until you were six, Timothy, and you were three, Rachel." *They really don't remember. How can that be? It seems like yesterday to me.* "Divorce hurts a lot," I said tearfully. "It is not God's plan, but He will help us through this. At times we will feel angry or sad or upset. That's okay. We can talk about it any time." They looked at me with innocent eyes, not comprehending my words. *Today is no different for them than any other day. Thank You, Lord, for cushioning them from some of this heartache. Help them grieve their own loss.*

After an eighteen-month separation, people weren't thinking about my situation. There was no easy way to broach the subject. I told a few friends, but I felt isolated in my grief.

A week after the court hearing, my friend Wes spoke to the Mothers' Bible Study group I attended. Fourteen years

ago, Wes and I had worked together in Christian education in area churches. After the study, I told him about my
day in court and the divorce. He listened and gave me
some advice. "Linda, go home and write a final letter to
Mark," he said. "This isn't a letter you will give him. Write
anything you still need to say to him. Be sure to forgive
him. After you've done that, I'll pray with you."

Writing that letter took days. Anger, hurt, pain, tears,
and forgiveness mingled together on the pages. After I finished it, I wrote another letter forgiving myself for how I
had contributed to our marriage failure. *Oh God, how desperately we both need Your love and forgiveness.*

I met with Wes a week later. He led me in a prayer of
forgiveness, release, and restoration. During our prayer
time, I sensed God's healing begin deep within my heart.
*Thank You, God, for bringing Wes across my path right after the
divorce. Thank You for his guidance and prayers during this
painful time in my life. Thank You for holding my life in Your
loving hands.*

### Relentless Needs

"Your AFDC grant, food stamps, and Medical
Assistance are terminated immediately," the letter from
the county stated. "Your household report form was not
turned in on time." *That's not true. I mailed it long before the
deadline. What's going on here?* I called my caseworker
immediately. She wasn't in. *Help me, God. These programs
are all we have to live on.*

After two days of frantic phone calling, I finally
reached her. After checking her records she said, "Your
report form is here. Your benefits will continue. Just ignore
that notice."

*They cut off all my financial help and then tell me to ignore the notice. This whole system is based on threats and control.* Roller-coaster emotions, round-the-clock responsibility for my children, and constant financial worries left me vulnerable and unstable. *What am I going to do? I don't have a plan for life after divorce.*

I applied for Energy Assistance, hoping to get help in paying our heating bills. "A grant is based on your income and utility bills from the past year," the worker explained. "This is one of the best grants I've seen all season! A credit of $431 will be sent to your utility companies."

*Wow! That'll go a long way to help pay our bills. The previous renters must have left their windows wide open all winter.*

"You also qualify for our free weatherization program," he explained. "Added insulation and weatherproofing will help reduce your future heating costs."

*Father, thank You for caring for us.*

Even though I limited all food purchases to food stamps, $125 could not feed the four of us each month. So I searched for more help. Monthly vouchers from Women, Infants, and Children (WIC) supplied us with orange juice, milk, cheese, and cereal. Once a month we got food from a local food shelf. As I asked for help, I remembered it was part of God's provision for us and received it gratefully.

I worried constantly about money. Even with my meticulous planning, $621 a month from AFDC didn't cover our basic needs. *I have ten dollars left until December— that's two weeks away! How long can I live like this? How can I tell anyone I have no money to put gas in my car? Somehow running out of money means I am a failure. I'm losing hope, Lord. Where are You in all of this?*

I carefully examined my projected budget for December. *After my tithe, regular bills, and two counseling sessions, I'll have seven dollars left for all other expenses for the whole month. No wonder I feel like I'm suffocating.* I began writing an itemized list of our needs:

**Timothy:** *warm red socks, shoes, underwear, long johns, winter coat, haircut*

**Rachel:** *pink winter boots, knee socks, underwear, long johns, tights, pink overalls, mittens, haircut*

**Jonathan**: *diapers, training pants, socks, undershirts, long johns, baby shampoo*

**Me:** *kneesocks, flannel nightgown, underwear, personal items, a battery for my watch, stamps, camera film, child care*

**Children's Supplies:** *glue, rubber cement, paper, washable markers, tape, construction paper*

**Household Items:** *napkins, dish soap, sandwich bags, aluminum foil, tissues, toilet paper, toothpaste, Children's Tylenol, laundry soap, car oil, windshield washer fluid*

When I completed the list, God quietly said, "Tell others your needs at this time." I can't do that, Lord. I'm afraid I'll be criticized for having these needs. I feel naked. I have no way to provide these things. God, You've promised to supply all our needs according to Your riches in Jesus. I trust You. Please protect my heart and give me grace to share these needs with others.

I called a woman from church and vaguely hinted

about my financial struggles. "The issue seems to be what *you* need to do," she concluded. "Even if you don't like it, you need to find some way to get more money. People are more willing to help if they see you really trying."

*I haven't been sitting around doing nothing. I'm writing and speaking to groups as God opens doors. I want to be home, caring for my children. I don't want to work full time outside my home. Am I wrong, Lord? I need a friend to understand what my life is like right now. We're not living extravagantly. This is bare-bones living; there are no luxuries to cut. I want someone to say, "Linda, you're doing the best you can in an extremely difficult situation."*

*Instead, I feel like others are judging me: "You're incompetent and irresponsible. No good mother would let her child's only shoes wear through and not replace them. What kind of a mother are you?" Since I barely make ends meet, somehow I am a failure.*

*Heavenly Father, I need someone to share my pain, someone to hold me and dry my tears, but no one is here. I feel so alone. I'm afraid You'll abandon me, too.*

"I get so discouraged," I told the Mothers' Bible Study group. "The Christmas season is hard to get through. I feel like I need a team of cheerleaders."

After the meeting, one mom said, "I'd like to pick up your children on Monday for supper and Christmas shopping. I've already bought some presents for them. I hope it's okay." She took them shopping and let them each pick out a gift for me. They ate pizza at her house and wrapped their presents. The few hours they were gone gave me a much-needed break. Another mom bought socks and underwear for my children. A family friend gave gifts and clothes to my children. She gave me "fun money" to spend on myself.

*Thank You, Lord, for these expressions of Your love. You are the only One with endless resources to help us. In these days when our needs seem limitless, help me trust You to meet them all.*

## Unexpected Support

My friend Wes and his wife Gretchen reached out to our family many times and included us in their family activities. I never felt like they looked down on me, even though they knew the details of my situation.

Gretchen called one day and gently asked, "How are you doing, Linda?"

"I can't keep living this way," I cried. "I'm continually worried about money. I can't bear the guilt when my children don't have winter boots or basic clothing they need."

"Linda," she replied, "you've been faithful in mothering your children." I burst into tears. "God sees your heart," she continued, "and He will reward you."

A stranger sent us a check for $150. *This is amazing! It will help us so much.* I called Wes and Gretchen and shared the good news.

"That businessman tries to bless one family each December," Wes said. "He asked us weeks ago if we knew a family in need. We gave him your name."

"Will you give me his address so I can thank him?" I asked.

"Sure."

I spent the money for my children's immediate needs and then wrote him a letter. "Your gift was an answer to my prayers," I wrote. "I bought boots, a winter coat, mittens, and clothes for my children. I thank God for your gift and for you."

A week later, Gretchen called. "The businessman read your note to his family," she said. "Now they all want to buy presents for your family. They would like to bring the gifts to our house, and we will bring them to you."

"Really?" I asked. "That would be wonderful."

Their gifts seemed handpicked for our family: a soft doll for Rachel, Lego bricks for Timothy, a toy drill for Jonathan, gift certificates for pizza, and movie passes. We never met the family who gave us those gifts, but we often thanked God for them and remembered their kindness to us.

A mechanic repaired my car and sent the bill with "PAID" scrawled across it. A phone rebate covered our current bill. A community group brought us a food basket plus handmade mittens for my children. My parents drove from Connecticut and my brother came from Kansas to spend Christmas with us. Blessings overflowed. I couldn't miss God's loving-kindness in all of it. *Thank You, Father, for Your abundant provision. Let Your love fill all the empty places in my heart.*

### Setting Priorities

I entered 1990 optimistically. God had sustained me through the heartbreak of separation and divorce. He was helping me make the transition into a new life. *Father, I want this year and this decade to be one of deepening intimacy with You. I want to know You as I never have before. Please increase my trust in You.*

A myriad of complicated formulas in the welfare regulations determined how any money I earned affected our assistance. When I reported the $100 I received for writing my first magazine article, my caseworker assured me it wouldn't affect our AFDC grant. But two months later, because of that income, our food stamps were reduced by twenty dollars. *I hate "surprises" like that. Why are there hidden penalties for earning money?*

From then on, I discussed each potential job with my caseworker to figure out its impact on our finances. I quickly learned the bottom line: when I earned money, either our AFDC grant or food stamps would be reduced.

*Why did I apply for welfare in the first place? Because I had no money. Why am I still on welfare almost two years later? Because I want to raise my own children. It means going without a lot of things, but at least my children have me.*

While sorting through the maze of welfare regulations, I reached two significant decisions: *I am not willing to work full time to get off the system, because that would require long-term day care for my children; and any part-time work I do must be personally satisfying, for it won't improve our financial situation much.*

My primary job was mothering my children. Nothing was more important to me. I viewed work options as opportunities to use my God-given abilities within the context of raising my family. Work needed to harmonize with nurturing my children, not preempt it. Writing and speaking both fit into this framework. An editor asked me to write more youth curriculum materials. I agreed. I only needed child care for Jonathan during Rachel's preschool classes to complete that assignment. Short-term projects suited my family priorities much better than long-term commitments. *Lord, You know our needs. You know the opportunities available for me to earn money. I commit our finances to You for 1990. I don't know what's ahead, but You are my provision.*

Shortly after completing that writing assignment, I received a notice from the county: "Census jobs are available. Income earned will not count against your AFDC grant or food stamps." *Here's a short-term job that can only benefit our family. Lord, if this is Your plan for me, please open the doors.*

"I have the opportunity to earn extra income by working for the Census Bureau during May," I told the Mothers' Bible Study group. "Would any of you be willing to help care for my children so I can do this?" Inwardly I feared someone would ask, "Why should *we* help *you*?" Instead, ten women volunteered! With their gracious help, I earned over $1000 during that hectic month. *God, You are so good. The census is only taken once every ten years. Thanks for providing this way for me to earn money for my family.*

I carefully analyzed how each potential job might affect our family's emotional and physical health. I needed to stay in balance to keep a stable atmosphere in our home. Daily I prayed for God's guidance about working. I considered several day care jobs but turned them down. An available job didn't automatically mean it was right for me. After interviewing for a position at a college, I realized it would require more time than I was willing to give.

Near the end of May, my friend Wes offered another option. "Linda," he asked, "would you consider working in our Paraclete Ministries office this summer, four mornings a week? My family would take care of your children, and I would pay some of your bills." This arrangement appeared to benefit all of us, so I accepted.

When summer ended, Wes and Gretchen gave me a bouquet of flowers and a gold necklace. "You are precious to God and to us," they said. "Thank you for your faithful service. It's been wonderful caring for your children, Linda, and you've been a big help to us in the ministry."

*Thank You, Father, for providing a job with people who love and appreciate my children and me.*

September 1990 marked one year since I'd started speaking and writing. To my surprise, I discovered that I had spoken fourteen times and completed four writing assignments. Five future commitments were already arranged. *Father, You are leading me. You are opening doors for me. Thank You for these satisfying ways of serving You and others while I nurture my children.*

### An Available Friend

"Linda, do you have someone to pray with?" Gretchen asked over the phone.

"Not really," I mumbled. This wasn't the first time she had asked me that question. I felt isolated, like I didn't belong anywhere. I experienced firsthand how divorce destroys social relationships. Friends faded away and new friendships hadn't yet formed. Loneliness engulfed me.

Gretchen's invitation—to meet together twice a month to talk and pray—boosted my spirit. I needed to talk about things I was facing. Even more, I needed someone to pray with me. Someone who would see God in my situation when I didn't; someone who could pray when I couldn't.

During our first meeting, Gretchen looked into my eyes and said, "Linda, I'm available to you for whatever you need. This is *your* time."

Tears welled up in my eyes. *No one has ever said that to me before.* And she meant it. Whatever I wanted to talk or pray about, that's what we did. It really was "my" time. As we met together, I heard God say, "Linda, I'm available for you, too."

Our conversations often focused on my struggles with work and the welfare system. "I keep trying to figure out how to get off the system," I said in frustration. "It's so complicated. I feel like a tiny bug caught in a huge spider web."

"God is using the welfare system as part of His provision for you," Gretchen reminded me. "*He* will get you off it in *His* time and in *His* way." Her words penetrated my heart. *Father, forgive me for carrying this welfare burden alone. You never meant it to be that way. I release it completely to You. I will trust You for Your plan and timing to get us off the system.*

As Gretchen and I met every other week, I learned to trust her with my feelings. "I can hardly drag myself out of bed in the morning," I confessed. "What's the point of getting up? I have no energy to care for my children. Sometimes I just sit and stare into space. I know I shouldn't feel this way, but it seems like my life is hopeless."

Gretchen listened and accepted my feelings. She also spoke encouraging words. "You have three beautiful children who need you, Linda," she said. "Keep on making meals for them. Keep reading to them. God will give you the strength you need to care for them each day."

When Gretchen and I met again, I shared the hopeless thoughts that filled my mind. Then she suggested, "Maybe it would help if I called you first thing in the morning and prayed with you. Would you like me to do that?"

"I guess so," I shrugged. "At least it would help get me up in the morning."

"What time?" she asked. "Is seven o'clock early enough?"

"Yeah, that's when I need to get up to help Timothy get ready for school."

"It won't be a time to talk, but a prayer to start the day."

The next morning the ringing phone woke me up. "Hello," I said groggily.

"Good morning, Linda!" Gretchen said cheerfully. "It's a beautiful day God has given us to be alive. Let's pray. Father, thank You for today and that You are always with us. Thank You for Your amazing love. Please wrap Linda in Your loving arms today. Let her know You care about every detail in her life. In Jesus' name. Amen." Tears slid down my cheeks as she prayed.

At 7:00 a.m. every morning, Gretchen called and prayed. She helped me start my day focused on God rather than my problems. Some days I didn't want to think about God. Some days I didn't feel like praying. But I always answered her early morning phone call. *Thank You, God, that Gretchen loves me and prays with me. Thank You that she's willing to walk with me through these depressing days.* Gretchen called every morning for more than six weeks. Her prayers planted seeds of thankfulness to God in my heart.

Gretchen also gave me strong support in being a mother. Committed to raising her own children, she valued that commitment in me. "Linda," she encouraged, "your first call after loving the Lord is to be a mother to your children. God honors your dedication to them and will bless you because of it."

Since Gretchen's children were older than mine, at times I sought her advice in handling situations at home. Over time, Dial-A-Mom got started. When I felt exasperated with my children or I wanted to resign as a mom, I'd call Gretchen. "Hi, I'm calling Dial-A-Mom. Is there a mother in the house?" That meant I needed to talk about an urgent issue. If she wasn't available, that message would alert her to call me as soon as possible. *Father, thank You for Gretchen's encouragement in raising my children. Thanks for her willingness to meet with me, listen to me, and pray with me. Thank You for her gentle love that shows itself in practical ways.*

## Words of Hope

Three times in 1990, God spoke specific words of hope to me exactly when I needed to hear them. The first time was the day in January I received final divorce papers in the mail. After reading them, I drove to a Christian leadership conference where I was scheduled to speak. Instead of sinking into depression, I spoke passionately of God's faithfulness and His provision for all our needs: the truth I desperately needed to hear that day. I returned home that evening, strengthened and encouraged by God.

The second time God clearly spoke to me was during the 1990 Christian Writers' Conference in Wheaton, Illinois. I attended the conference to improve my writing skills and receive encouragement as a writer. God had much more planned.

"The place to begin all writing is on your knees," one speaker emphasized. "Writing flows from the overflow of God's life in you." *Father, I want everything I write to give life and stir others to depend more fully on You.*

"The greatest Author in the universe, Almighty God, lives within you," another speaker reminded us. "He possesses the most creative mind and the most sensitive heart in the world. Think big," he challenged, "bigger than you've ever thought before."

During my time alone with God the next morning, He quietly spoke. "Linda, someday you will write a book about your life and My provision."

*Father, that's far beyond anything I've ever considered. I'm totally inadequate.*

Then I remembered the wise advice from the speakers the previous day. It helped me focus on God's greatness, not my smallness. *Father, I'm willing to be Your instrument to communicate Your message to others. In Your time, I'm trusting You to give me:*

> *the desire to write a book*
> *the joy and anticipation of writing a book*
> *a vision for the book*
> *a focused audience for the book*
> *a plan for the book*
> *the words for the book*
> *an editor/publisher for the book.*

God's peace enveloped me as I placed "the book" completely in His hands.

God also spoke words of encouragement to me one afternoon in August. My heart ached as I watched my three children climb into their father's car and ride away to his wedding rehearsal. *God, please help me through this painful time.* Ten minutes later the phone rang. "I'm calling about the article you submitted about the Mothers' Bible Study group," the magazine editor said. "We want to publish it and will pay you $150."

As I hung up the phone, I heard God's voice of encouragement. "Linda, I have plans for you. Good plans. I'm here with you to lead and guide you."

### A Safe Place

Wes and Gretchen invited us to join their family for various activities. We spent Mother's Day with them, enjoyed cookouts in their backyard, went sledding, and celebrated holidays together. They helped us laugh again and build new family memories. Their genuine love and kindness deeply touched my heart.

During one get-together, I told them about the ongoing problems with my upstairs neighbors. "Blaring music upstairs drowns out conversations in our home," I explained. "People stomp up and down the hallway stairs during all hours of the night."

"Come over to our house when you need to get away," they offered. "Just call and see if we're here."

One night in October 1990, a moving truck pulled up to our back door. Four more people moved into the duplex above us, bringing the total to ten. I notified the owner the next morning. He wasn't aware of the situation and thanked me for calling. He confronted the renters and told them the date they would all need to move out.

Conflicts escalated. They didn't care about violating city housing codes. They blamed me for informing the owner and made my life miserable. Ten people walking and running around above us created a constant racket in our home. Then the woman upstairs threatened me. Several times water from upstairs dripped down through our bathroom ceiling. One morning my kitchen cupboard and all its food items were soaked with water from their overflowed kitchen sink. *I can't stand this. I'm becoming a nervous wreck. Help me, God.* The renters didn't move out by the deadline, so the owner started eviction proceedings. He asked me to appear in court as a witness.

One evening we "escaped" to Wes and Gretchen's for a few hours of peace. I updated them on our three-month conflict. "Sometimes I don't feel safe at home with my children,"

I explained. "I never know what our upstairs neighbors will do. People come and go from their place all night long."

"Linda, you're welcome here anytime, day or night," Wes and Gretchen said, as they handed me a key.

"You're giving me a key to your house?" I exclaimed, turning it over in my hands. "We can really come any time?" *I can hardly believe this. You have to trust someone a lot to give them a key to your house.*

"There's no need to call," Wes and Gretchen assured me. "Just come. Anytime. Let our home be a safe place for you and your children."

Several times we took refuge in their home. Once we stayed overnight. *Thank You, God, for Wes and Gretchen. Thanks for this safe place to come to. Thank You for providing for our needs.*

The upstairs neighbors moved out the night before their eviction date. *Finally, my children and I are alone in a quiet house.* The constant strain I'd been under slowly began to lift. During January, while the upstairs duplex was being repaired, I gradually began to relax in my own home. *Thank You, God, for protecting us through these difficult months. Now we have a peaceful home again. You are caring for us.*

### Intense Loneliness

I hadn't seen my friend Carol in months. College classes and her family's needs filled her days. Now and then we talked on the phone, but we couldn't get together regularly like we had two years ago.

I appreciated Wes and Gretchen and the time they spent with me. They helped me physically, emotionally, and spiritually. Yet an emptiness deep within me still cried out to be filled.

I ached for an everyday kind of friend. Someone I could see and touch and tell about the daily happenings in my home. Someone who would rejoice with me in my children's accomplishments and laugh at the funny things they said. Someone I could share my thoughts and feelings with. *God, please give me that kind of friend.*

God gently kept saying, "Get to know Me more. I long to be your closest companion, your dearest friend." But I kept turning away. I built barricades around my heart to keep Him at a distance. He continued calling, "Linda, come away with Me. Come to Me to be refreshed. Let Me love you. Let Me embrace you. I have much to say to you. Come and be alone with Me today." He lovingly invited me, but I was afraid. Afraid of getting too close to Him. Afraid of being hurt.

*Lord, I'm afraid of intimacy with You. I'm afraid to trust You with my emotional needs. I'm afraid You'll abandon me. Forgive me for turning away from Your open arms. Forgive me for believing You can't meet my needs. Please melt my heart and help me respond to Your love.*

As I spent time with the Lord daily, He began revealing Himself to me. I got to know Him as He is revealed in the Bible, particularly as my Heavenly Father. *You're so different from what I thought You were like, Father.* He said, "I have loved you with an everlasting love; I have drawn you with loving-kindness" (Jeremiah 31:3). I began to picture myself as a child sitting on His lap. As He wrapped His arms around me, I soaked up His gentle love for me.

After months of spending time with God, my prayers changed. *Father, Your tender love for me is far beyond any love this world can give. I long to know You more intimately. I want to grow closer to You. Please stir up in me an unquenchable desire for You. I love You.*

## At the Grave Site

Intense feelings stirred within me during a funeral in September 1991. We had watched the laughter and life drain out of our pastor's wife during her long, debilitating illness. At her memorial service, everyone celebrated her life and rejoiced that she was with Jesus. To my surprise, I found myself comparing her funeral with my divorce. *That was two years ago. Why are such strong feelings erupting now? And why here?*

I decided to go to the grave site. Unable to find anyone to ride with, I drove alone. I burst into tears on the way there. *What's going on? This is about more than my friend's death.* I watched from a distance as her entire family and many friends gathered around her grave. I cried harder. I hurried back to my car and sobbed uncontrollably.

Later at the church reception, expressions of love and comfort surrounded our pastor. *There was no reception for me after my day in court. I drove home alone and cried alone. Many will keep in touch with our pastor in the coming months to see how he's doing. After my divorce, there were no phone calls.*

A deep sadness hung over me for days. "Somehow I feel like I'm crying over the death of my marriage," I told Gretchen when we met together. "I don't understand what's going on inside of me," I said, as tears slid down my cheeks. "The loneliness I feel is more than I can stand."

"I know this sounds trite, Linda," she replied, "but Jesus was there with you." Her words made me cry harder.

The next day, I spent extended time alone with God and brought my heartache to Him. *Father, please help me face these feelings. Show me the truth.*

This scene quickly flashed through my mind: *I'm driving alone to the cemetery to the burial of my marriage. The greatest pain I feel is that I'm totally alone. No one else has come with me to witness the burial. No one is here to comfort or support me. No one is here to encourage me or reassure me of God's love. The total loneliness is almost too much to bear. I leave alone, drive home alone, and cry alone. God, how I hurt inside.*

Then I saw the same scene differently: *I'm driving to the cemetery to the burial of my marriage. Jesus is sitting in the front seat with me. He doesn't say a word, but His eyes convey that He feels my pain. When we arrive, He takes my hand and walks with me to the grave site. He puts His strong arm around me as we stand there, and I notice tears in His eyes.*

*My pain is so deep. I feel like I'm being ripped into pieces and part of me is dying and being buried. I begin to sob uncontrollably. Jesus turns to me and I bury my head in His shoulder as He gently and compassionately holds me close. I cry there by the grave site for a long, long time. I cry about my broken hopes and dreams. I cry in anger that I could not stop the divorce from happening. I cry over the responsibility of caring for my three small children. I cry about my fears of the future. I cry over the searing pain of rejection in my heart. I cry that my life is in shambles. I cry until I am exhausted.*

*As I slowly begin to calm down, I realize that Jesus has been crying all along with me. Somehow He feels my anguish, my despair, my loss. I know I need to leave, yet I feel like I can't go on. Then Jesus gently cups my face in His hands. His deep loving eyes look right into mine, and He softly says, "I will never leave you or forsake you."*

*He tenderly picks me up and carries my lifeless body to the car. He drives me home, carries me into the house, and helps me get comfortable so I can rest. He is always available. In the middle of the night, when I toss and turn, He gently puts His hand on my shoulder to calm me. When I feel such tremendous anger that I could scream, He listens as I pour out my heart. When I am overwhelmed with caring for my children, He gives me the grace and strength to go on. When the hurt and loneliness close in on me, He holds me close and comforts me.*

*Slowly, very slowly, I begin to regain my strength. But I in no way outgrow my deep need for Jesus. I continue to heal deep within because of Jesus' continual presence and His abiding love for me.*

\* \* \*

1. Do you have an "available friend" to talk and pray with? If yes, how has he or she been a blessing in your life? If not, how could one benefit you at this time?

2. What do you worry about? Be specific. What is God's remedy for worry according to Philippians 4:6-7? How does that work in your life?

3. How do you handle feelings of loneliness? "God has said, 'Never will I leave you; never will I forsake you'" (Hebrews 13:5). How can God's promise help you when you feel utterly alone?

*Father, at times I've felt abandoned by others. I've even felt abandoned by You. Help me believe You are always with me, no matter how I feel.*

## Chapter Three

# God Is For Me

*This I know, that God is for me*
(Psalm 56:9, NASB).

### *Breaking New Ground*

Carol, Jim, and their children, our missionary friends from Japan, became avid campers during their three-year stay in the United States. My family spent a sunny summer afternoon with them and their pop-up camper at a nearby campground. *I like the relaxed pace out here and the simplicity of life. Maybe someday my children and I could learn to camp. It would be something new for us that would build family memories.*

"What will you do with your camper when you return to Japan in a few months?" I asked.

"We'll probably sell it," they replied, "since we'll only come back here to visit every two years."

Before we left their campsite, I surprised myself by saying, "Let me know if you decide to sell the camper. I might want to buy it so we can learn to camp."

A few weeks later, Timothy and I met with Jim about the camper. He demonstrated how easy it was to put up and take down. Timothy's obvious interest ignited something within me. *Timothy and I could lift the camper shell. Rachel and Jonathan could help with the sides. I'm sure we'd be able to set it up by ourselves.*

"We want to sell the camper for $500," Jim said, "so let us know soon if you want to buy it. We'll also sell our other camping equipment separately."

"I'm very interested," I replied. "I need to find out if my Chevy Citation can pull it. I'll call you in a few days."

I couldn't stop thinking about that camper. When I told Wes about it, he shared stories about a camper they had owned years before. "We took great trips with it when our boys were young," he reminisced. "You'd have fun with a camper, Linda." *We could have wonderful family times with it. But why am I even considering this? Buying the camper would use all my savings.*

A few days later, I stopped back at Wes's house. "I'm so disappointed," I lamented. "My Citation can't pull the weight of the camper. This adventure ended before it even began."

"Gretchen and I have been talking about that camper since you were here the other day," Wes replied. "We'd like to take our girls camping. How about if we buy it together?"

"But my car can't pull it," I repeated.

"You could borrow our van when you want to camp, and we'd use your car."

"You would do that?"

"Sure, why not? We've got room to store it next to our garage, so it would be kept in a protected place. What do you think?"

"Wes, I don't know how to drive pulling a camper. I don't know why I even considered doing this. The whole idea is crazy."

"No, it's not, Linda," Wes assured me. "I can teach you how to back up and turn with the camper. Your family would have so much fun with it."

A few weeks later, we bought the camper together. Wes taught me how to hitch the camper to their van and drive with it. I practiced backing the camper into their driveway. I knew I had to be comfortable driving with the camper before we could travel anywhere. *Father, thanks for Wes and Gretchen. They encourage me to try new things and help me do them. I know You have fun times planned for our family.*

To celebrate my fortieth birthday, we "camped out" in Wes's driveway. His family set up the camper for us before leaving town for the weekend. My children and I roasted hot dogs and sang songs. We giggled as we played with our flashlights inside the camper in the dark. Timothy, Rachel, and Jonathan, ages ten, seven, and five, loved their first taste of camping. The next day we took the camper down and put it away, by following directions I had written out. Our first campout was a huge success!

A few weeks later we camped at a county park. The first night we were eaten alive by a swarm of mosquitoes that found its way inside the camper through a tiny opening. We returned home three days later with innumerable bites and funny stories about Rachel, the "mosquito bite queen," and Timothy, the "mosquito masher." We also brought back wonderful memories of hunting for treasures, making campfires, swimming, and building sand sculptures. Our family camping adventures had begun.

*Thank You, Father, for the courage to try something I've never done before. You are helping us build fun family memories.*

### Continuous Worry

Worry held me hostage. *Will my children have enough food to eat this month? How am I going to pay for Timothy and Rachel's school supplies? What if our car breaks down?* One day I read in my Bible, "Do not be anxious about anything, but in everything, by prayer and petition, with thanksgiving, present your requests to God" (Philippians 4:6). *I memorized that verse years ago. Don't worry about anything. Pray about everything.*

Suddenly I realized how much time and energy I wasted by worrying. *Father, I worry about almost everything. I churn inside instead of turning to You. Please forgive me. I don't want to be like this. Please set me free from this lifetime habit of worrying. Teach me to trust You.*

My car gave me ample opportunities to trust God, especially when the back brakes went out. *Father, You said not to worry. You told me to bring my needs to You with thankfulness. Thank You for how You will provide the money for these repairs.*

After fixing the brakes, the mechanic advised, "I wouldn't put any more money into this Citation if I were you. Repairs will only get more costly. You'd be better off looking for a different car." *Father, help me trust You.*

I still owed money for the brake repairs and the car insurance payment was nearly due. An unexpected check came in the mail. A few days later, I received a note with a check for seventy-five dollars. Seeing God provide for these specific needs stirred me to pray boldly. *Father, You provided our Citation. You know which car would be best for us in the future and how to finance it. You know when I should sell this car and buy another one. I commit it all to You. Please guide me to our next car. Help me trust You.*

For several weeks I left the car situation in God's hands. Then I decided to take action. *If I don't search for a car, we'll never get one. Help, Lord. I don't trust car salesmen. I don't want them trying to take advantage of me.*

The day before I intended to look at used cars, Jonathan came down with chicken pox. Then Timothy; then Rachel. I was homebound for six weeks! Worries tormented me daily. *Father, I've had no car payments for two years, but I barely make ends meet. How can I possibly afford to buy a car? You know we need a reliable one. I'm trusting You.*

While my children were recovering from chicken pox, my friend Wes called. "Linda, I'm wondering if you'd be interested in buying my car. This white '87 Dodge Aries is in excellent condition, but it has high mileage. Since you mostly drive locally, I thought it might work well for you. How about if we exchange cars for a week so you can see if you like it?"

We traded cars. I immediately liked his little white car. *Father, this is a new option. Is this Your plan for our next car? You know our needs. I'm trusting You.*

Since we received financial assistance through AFDC, I called my caseworker about the car. "According to AFDC regulations, an '87 Dodge Aries is too good of a car," he told me. "If you buy it, your AFDC grant will immediately be cut off."

"So what kind of car *can* I buy?" I snapped. "One that's broken down and needs constant repair?"

The caseworker ended our heated discussion, saying, "You can lease any car you want, but you cannot buy one over a certain value." *That does me a lot of good. Leasing costs more money and the car isn't mine.*

I slowly drove Wes's car back to his house. "Wes, I like your car a lot, but if I buy it, I'll lose my AFDC grant," I reported glumly. "The rules are so dumb. My caseworker said I can lease any car, but AFDC has strict regulations about owning cars. It seems like they want me to drive an old dilapidated junker."

"Then I'll lease this car to you," Wes said immediately.

"What?"

"We can work out some arrangement," he encouraged. "Keep using the car for a few more days and we'll talk again."

Later that week, Wes's early morning phone call woke me up. "I've got a buyer for your Citation," he said. "They'll pay $300, and they want to buy it this morning."

"I can't sell my car," I protested. "Then I won't have one."

"You can keep using the little white car for now," Wes reassured me.

*Three hundred dollars is a good price for my car. Selling it now would eliminate the hassle of trying to sell it myself. But what about a car for my family?* With mixed emotions I replied, "Tell them I'll sell it."

For days I regretted my decision. *Now I've sold my car and I have no guarantees about the Dodge Aries. What if Wes wants more money than I can pay? I'll end up with no car at all.* I drove his white car to my friend's auto shop to have it checked over. *Wes might be trying to sell me a lemon. Why else would he be so interested in leasing it to me? Father, Wes has only been kind and helpful to me, but it's hard for me to trust him. It's hard to trust any man. It's even hard to trust You.*

After two agonizing weeks of waiting, Wes and I finally met to discuss details. With the sale of my old car plus my small savings, I was still $500 short of the price he was asking. *This is exactly what I was afraid of. Now I'm stuck. Why did I ever sell that Citation?*

"You can pay the $500 whenever you are able," Wes said. "Not only do I want to lease this car to you, Linda, I also want to maintain it. You can pay a monthly fee to cover car insurance and basic repairs, and I will service it for you. *I can't believe this! It sounds too good to be true!*

Wes's eyes sparkled. "I've got it!" he exclaimed. "We can call the company Promised Land Motors!" Looking directly into my eyes, Wes said, "Linda, we want this to work for you. Gretchen and I want you to know how much we love you and support you. This car is an expression of God's love for you."

*Father, when Wes and I first traded cars a month ago, You already knew Your car plans for us. I was driving our new car before I knew it was mine! How good You are! How wonderfully You care for me in spite of my doubts and worries.*

### Gratitude

Rachel delighted in her year of preschool (1989-90), a gift from Bobbie. Then Bobbie gave my son Jonathan a scholarship to attend preschool twice a week. In 1991, when his school year was almost over, she paid his preschool tuition for three afternoons a week for the following year. Rachel and Jonathan eagerly attended preschool. They each loved learning more about Jesus and singing songs about Him. They both spoke of Bobbie as the person who gave them the gift of preschool. *Thank You, Father, for Bobbie's generous investment in Rachel and Jonathan's lives.*

Raising my three children alone exhausted me. Divorce proceedings, continual financial struggles, and conflicts with our upstairs neighbors sapped my strength. Fears about the unknown future assailed me.

Bobbie's gift of preschool helped me through those difficult three years. The hours Rachel or Jonathan spent in preschool gave me a much-needed break from round-the-clock parenting. Once Jonathan started preschool, I had five-to-seven hours of uninterrupted time each week. I spent time alone with God, ran errands alone, made phone calls, and went to appointments. *Thank You, Father, for these hours to try and put my life back together.*

During those three years, I often felt totally depleted, with nothing inside to give my children. I longed to provide a peaceful, nurturing atmosphere in my home, but daily life seemed chaotic. When I took my children to preschool and left them in the care of the two Christian teachers, tears of gratitude often filled my eyes. I knew that, for those few hours, Rachel or Jonathan would be loved and cared for in a peaceful, stable setting. *Thank You, Father, for these two women who welcome and treasure my children as their own. Thank You for their kind words, their gentle touch, their devotion to You, and their genuine love. Thank You for loving my children through them today.*

### Gentle Guidance

Jonathan started kindergarten in September 1992. Many moms couldn't wait for their children to start school; I wished mine could stay home. I choked back tears as he climbed on the bus.

While he was in school, I prepared for my speaking and teaching commitments. I also took a class at ACTS, a local

Bible college, to help me teach God's Word more effectively.

With Jonathan in school, I felt pressured to get a full-time job. Others communicated, directly or indirectly, that I should be providing for my family and that I was irresponsible to turn down any job in my field. *Father, more than anything, I want to follow as You lead me. I'm waiting for Your direction for my life.*

In October, I was interviewed at a nearby church for a position as Director of Christian Education, my profession before my children were born. *Father, what are Your plans for our family at this time? You've given me abundant joy in mothering my children. I place my heart's desire to stay home with them in Your hands.*

The church offered me the job: twenty hours a week at ten dollars an hour. *Father, how do I decide about this job?* "I'm so confused," I told Gretchen. "This job is in my field and it's an opportunity to earn money. But I'm afraid of making a wrong choice."

"Linda, what do you really want to do?" she asked.

"I want my children to remain top priority," I replied immediately. "I want to give my best to them."

After we prayed together, Gretchen hugged me. "Linda, I support you in whatever decision you make."

"Your children need to see you working," another person insisted. "You need to get out and do something." *What do you think I've been doing these past four years? Father, I want to follow Your plans. Please reveal them to me.*

I called my caseworker about the job. "If you take it," she said, "your AFDC grant will end and food stamps will be reduced. Once you're off AFDC, you will receive child-support payments." I learned my rent portion would increase. I estimated costs for child care. *This system doesn't* make sense. *If I take this job, we'll have less money to live on than we do now. What should I do, Lord?*

A week later, I still had no inner peace or clear direction from God. I turned down the job. *Father, I don't know what's up ahead. Please open other doors for me. Help me trust You.*

I considered taking additional classes at ACTS. *If I'm going to take more classes, why not enroll in the two-year degree program?* I wrestled with that thought for weeks. My primary argument against enrolling was the mission trip requirement. *There's no way I could leave the country on a mission trip when I have three young children at home. Anyway, how could I pay the school tuition?* To all my inner questioning, God's response seemed to be, "Just enroll, and leave the rest to Me."

In January 1993, still questioning how I could ever complete the program, I registered as a part-time student. I took three classes and studied while my children were in school.

Suddenly I started receiving numerous invitations to speak and teach in area churches. The churches sent any honorarium to ACTS toward my tuition and books. This procedure conformed to welfare regulations, so our AFDC grant was not reduced. *God, You are so creative in providing this means to pay my school expenses. I joyfully abandon myself to You. I trust You with my life, my children, and my future.*

### Enlarged Vision

Soon after classes started at ACTS, I noticed a flyer on the school bulletin board:

**Mission Trip to Mexico**
*July 9-18, 1993*
*ACTS students ~ Singles*
*Single parents and their children*
*All are welcome*

*I never thought about all of us going on a mission trip! Lord, we could serve You as a family and meet my school requirements too.* My excitement grew daily as I learned more about the trip. The team, led by Youth With a Mission (YWAM), would travel thirty-six hours by bus to Monterrey, Mexico, and spend seven days reaching out to people with God's love.

*Father, I've never gone on a mission trip. I can hardly believe I'm thinking about it! I know this mission outreach would be life changing for our family. The cost is more than our monthly AFDC grant. There's no way we can save that amount of money in four months. But I believe You could provide that amount if You want us to go.*

Several days later, I asked my children, "What would you think about our family going on a mission trip to Mexico this summer?"

"Really? Do you mean it? That would be great, Mom!" they exclaimed. "When would we go? Where would we stay? What would we do there?" Their enthusiasm grew with each answer I gave.

"Let's pray together," I encouraged them. "Father, please show us if You want our family to serve You in Mexico this summer. Thanks for Your good plans for us."

After praying for another week, I felt confident of God's leading. "I believe God wants us to serve Him in Mexico this summer," I told my children.

"Yeah!" they exclaimed. "When do we go?" Then they grew quiet. "Mom, how will we get the money for the trip?"

"Let's ask God," I replied. "Father, we want to be Your missionaries in Mexico this summer. Please provide the $775 we need for this outreach. Nothing is too hard for You."

We sent letters to relatives and friends, asking for prayer and financial support. Daily we checked our mailbox. Each response strengthened our trust in God.

Timothy, Rachel, and Jonathan, ages eleven, eight, and six, expressed interest in different areas of the outreach. Rachel gathered clothes she had outgrown to give to Mexican children. Jonathan couldn't wait to give out Bibles. Timothy wanted to help build a church. They all learned mime skits with the other children on our team.

By late May, God provided $805, and many people to pray for us. In June, my children and I each walked ten miles on our team walkathon and raised over $200. *Thank You, Father. This money will pay our food expenses while traveling, and provide money for projects during the outreach.* God provided another $300 before we left.

"God really wants us to go on this trip," my children agreed. "Now we have lots of money to give to the people in Mexico." *Father, thank You for Your abundant provision.*

As we prepared to leave, all kinds of doubts and worries flooded my mind. *Father, so much of this mission trip is unknown to me. I commit the entire trip to you: every detail, every situation, every need. Help me lean on You continually.*

Our team combined with another team and traveled by bus to Mexico. We all stayed at an orphanage. During our second day there, a majestic mountain range suddenly appeared. It had been totally hidden behind thick clouds. "Look at those mountains," I exclaimed. "They're breathtaking! When they're hidden by the clouds, you'd never even know they were there."

Quietly, God spoke to my heart. "I am with you all the time, Linda. Sometimes you sense My presence, sometimes you don't. My presence doesn't depend on what you see or feel, but on My Word. I have promised to never leave you or forsake you. I am always with you." That truth comforted me as I faced many unfamiliar situations in Mexico. Those mountains reminded me of God's presence.

During the mission trip, I thought I would be like a mother hen, carefully watching over her chicks. Not so. Instead, I learned many lessons about releasing my children. Timothy stayed in the dormitory for the men and boys, far down the hill from us. My children and I each worked at different sites when our team spent an entire day doing construction work in a very poor area.

My children each joined different Bible distribution teams. God gave me abundant grace to let them go with people I barely knew, into a foreign city, to tell others about Jesus in Spanish. Whenever I felt anxious about my children, I looked at the mountains and remembered that God was with each of us.

After giving out Bibles each afternoon, the teams met together to share their stories. One day God used Rachel to lead a woman to Jesus. The next day, God used me to lead someone to Him. *Father, You work through us though we hardly speak the language! You only ask us to be willing servants.*

The children on our team performed mimes at outreaches in parks and at a church. Without words they clearly expressed God's love for all people. I helped lead worship throughout the week. At one service, through an interpreter, I shared my testimony of God's faithfulness to our family. *Father, I never thought I'd get to tell people in another country how good You are! Thank You for bringing our family here to declare Your faithfulness.*

God deeply touched our family through our Mexico mission trip. We saw how He generously provided for all our needs. We witnessed people coming to know Jesus through our halting Spanish. We shared our faith through mime, music, and testimony. We helped with hands-on construction. We worked and worshiped with the Mexican Christians. We shared the joy of giving money toward specific projects.

*Father, You are an awesome God. Thank You for providing this opportunity to serve You as a family in another country while my children are so young. Please grow the seeds for missions that You planted in our hearts on this trip.*

### Childlike Faith

"When can we fly to see Grandma and Grandpa?" Jonathan asked a few weeks after our Mexico mission trip.

"I don't know," I replied. My parents lived in Connecticut, too far for me to drive. Airplane tickets were far beyond our meager budget. In 1988 and 1992, they had bought tickets for us to fly out to visit them.

"I want us to go see them again," he insisted.

"It costs a lot of money," I emphasized.

"How much money?" Jonathan persisted.

"A lot more than we have."

"Then we can save up for it," he decided. Over the next few weeks he often asked us, "Do you have any money to contribute for our trip?" and held open an envelope with "Connecticut" printed on it. "When can we fly to Grandma and Grandpa's?" he asked every few days.

Rachel wrote a report for school about our 1992 trip to Grandma and Grandpa's. Then all three children started sharing stories about that trip and what they liked best.

"Can we go again soon, Mom?" they all asked.

*It would be fun, but it's not possible.*

"Look at all this money in our envelope!" Jonathan exclaimed in early December. In four months he'd saved three dollars. "Now can we fly to Grandma and Grandpa's?" Jonathan pleaded.

"It costs much more than three dollars," I replied dismally. *He's so intent on going, but I don't see how it could happen. I don't have money for a trip to Connecticut. I don't have money for any kind of trip anywhere.*

Unexpected gifts that Christmas abundantly met all our immediate needs. *Maybe that $100 bill among the gifts we received could go toward a trip to my parents.* Without telling my children, I set that $100 aside, and determined to quickly save as much money for the trip as possible.

In January, I set aside fifty dollars. In February, I set aside sixty-five dollars from our regular living expenses. In March, I set aside $100 from our budget for the trip. With a monthly income of $621, my "trip savings plan" created tremendous stress. *I feel like I'm strangling myself. But if I don't keep saving like this, how will we ever go?*

I asked friends to pray with me about the possibility of this trip, but I couldn't pray boldly myself. *What if I count on God and He doesn't come through? How would that affect my children's faith?* By mid March, I was ready to give up on the whole idea. *Father, You know we want to go. I'm tired of trying to make this trip happen. I can't do it. I surrender the entire trip to You—the money, the timing, whether we go at all.*

As I gave up all my plans, something changed inside of me. God planted the faith in my heart for the trip. *He would work a miracle for us.*

The next day I gathered my children together. "Let's pray specifically about a trip to Grandma and Grandpa's," I encouraged.

"Dear God," Timothy said earnestly, "please let there be discount plane tickets on sale this summer."

"For $1000 or less," Rachel added.

"And show us ways to earn the money," Jonathan prayed.

"Help us trust You," I pleaded.

From that moment on, the trip became a family adventure of faith. We had $315, plus five dollars from Jonathan's "trip envelope." The next day, a student in my class at ACTS gave me a check for thirty dollars. "This is from three of us," he said. "We don't know what it's for. Sorry for the delay in getting it to you."

*This is trip money!* A few days later, I qualified for a consumer taste test that paid fifteen dollars. *More trip money.*

In April, I asked students at ACTS to pray with me about the trip. As we prayed, my inner conflict emerged. *Lord, this trip is not like the Mexico mission trip to help others. It seems selfish to ask You to provide so we can visit my parents.*

During my time alone with God the following day, I read Luke 18. Jesus met the blind man and asked, "What do you want Me to do for you?" The blind man answered, "Lord, I want to regain my sight."

Tears came to my eyes as I sensed Jesus asking me, "Linda, what do you want *Me* to do for *you?*"

I quickly replied, "I'd like four tickets to Connecticut this summer and the money to pay for them." When I spoke those words, it seemed like Jesus wrote it down and checked it off as already completed. I knew in my heart it was done. *Father, Your love overwhelms me.*

The next day I excitedly told Pam, a friend at ACTS, how Jesus had revealed Himself to me in my quiet time. She could hardly wait until I finished to share her good news.

"Randy [her husband] and I prayed," she said, "and we both felt God prompting us to be part of this trip. We want you to receive this check as from the Lord." The amount was $500!

My children were ecstatic when I told them how God had answered our prayers. "Now we have over $800," Jonathan exclaimed. "Soon we'll be able to go."

"Let's sell pop and homemade cookies at our annual garage sale," Rachel suggested. We raised twenty-six dollars! *More trip money.* Throughout the spring months, our family prayed together about the trip. We thanked God for the money He had already provided and trusted Him for the rest.

By the end of April, we had $1,052. The lowest-priced tickets cost $1,164. We continued praying, confident that somehow God would provide the remaining $112. In May, Rent Assistance sent me a letter: "The ceiling limit for rent has been raised, so your portion of the rent will be reduced. Starting June 1, your rent payment will *decrease* $113 per month!" *God, only You could make that happen right now. Your timing is perfect.*

In August, one year after Jonathan began asking to go, we flew to Connecticut and spent two weeks with Grandma and Grandpa. We told them how God miraculously answered our prayers and provided the money for the trip. With Grandma and Grandpa we explored an airplane museum, toured a submarine, swam in the ocean, and spent a day in a colonial village. We played miniature golf together. We picked blueberries. We ate homemade ice cream at a nearby ice cream shop twice. We enjoyed fourteen fun-filled, memory-building, action-packed days together.

This "faith trip" taught me an important lesson: God can use the youngest member of the family to unfold His plans. *Father, You put this trip in Jonathan's heart. Thank You for his persistence and his childlike trust in You. Thanks for helping me hear Your voice through him.*

### Overflowing Love

A few days before Christmas, our doorbell rang. When I opened the door, a woman I didn't know cheerfully called out "Merry Christmas!" and walked inside with a pile of gifts. She placed the beautifully wrapped presents on the floor beside seven-year-old Jonathan. "God loves you, Jonathan," she said softly and patted his head. Another woman carried in gifts, too. Before I could figure out what was happening, they returned with armloads of more gifts in all shapes and sizes.

"Have a wonderful Christmas, Timothy," one woman said as she looked into his eyes. "God loves you." Within minutes, they returned with more gifts.

"Rachel, God loves you so much," one said, gently squeezing her shoulder.

My children's eyes bulged at the stacks of gifts all over our living room floor. *Who are these people? I'm sure I don't know them. How do they know us? Where did all these gifts come from?* My questions remained unasked and unanswered as the two women scurried about.

Next, they carried a huge box of food into the kitchen. They hurried in with an ice chest filled with frozen foods and a turkey. They both gave me a big hug, and said, "God bless you, Linda. He loves you very much."

As they dashed out the front door, they waved and joyfully exclaimed, "Have a wonderful Christmas! God loves you all. God bless you." And they were gone.

I stood, dazed, gazing at the piles of gifts and the abundance of food. Tears streamed down my cheeks. At that moment, God whispered to me, "Linda, this is how I love you all the time: extravagantly, abundantly, joyfully. My love for you is very personal. I *am* caring for you and your children." Waves of His love washed over me.

"Mom, Mom," my children asked, pulling on my sleeves, "do you know those people?"

"I've never seen so many presents in our house," Timothy exclaimed.

"How did they know our names?" Rachel questioned.

"Look at all the presents with my name on them," Jonathan squealed with delight.

Overcome with emotion, I tenderly gathered my children in my arms. "This is a picture of what God's love is like," I said softly, with a sense of wonder. "He loves each one of us very, very much."

\* \* \*

1. In what area of your life has God recently given you clear direction? God promises to instruct us (Psalm 32:8) and give wisdom to all who ask (James 1:5). Did He guide you through His Word, people, circumstances, or an inner knowing?

2. Describe a time when God communicated His love to you in a special way.

3. "For I am the LORD, your God, who takes hold of your right hand and says to you, Do not fear; I will help you" (Isaiah 41:13). What evidence do you have that God is *for* you in your life right now? How is He helping you?

*Father, please give me faith to believe: You are on my side, You are eager to help me, and You are constantly caring for me.*

## Chapter Four

# God Restores My Hope

*May the God of hope fill you with all joy and peace as you trust in him, so that you may overflow with hope by the power of the Holy Spirit* (Romans 15:13).

### Just the Right Size

I watched seven-year-old Jonathan as he struggled to ride Rachel's old bike. *That bike won't work for him this year. His knees hit the handlebars each time he pedals. I hope we can find a bigger one at a garage sale. Ten dollars is all I can spare.*

At bedtime, Jonathan said, "Mom, I need a bigger bike. That one's too small."

"It sure is," I agreed. "Jonathan, do you remember what we've been learning about praying specifically?"

"Yeah," he nodded. "We tell God exactly what we'd like so we know when He answers our prayers."

"Let's pray that way for a bike. What's most important about a bike for you?'"

"That it's just my size," he answered immediately.

"How about the color?"

"Any color's fine. I can always paint it. I want it to be my size."

"How about the seat or the style of bike?"

"It doesn't matter. I just want it to be my size."

"Then let's talk to God about it now," I encouraged.

"Dear God," Jonathan began, "my bike is too small and I need a different one. I want a bike that's just my size."

"Dear God," I prayed, "You know what Jonathan's size is. You know what bike is best for him. Please show us where to look for his new bike. Thanks that You will provide it at just the right time. We love you. Amen."

I gave Jonathan a big hug and whispered, "Good night. I love you."

As I walked out of his room, Jonathan asked, "Mom, can we go to garage sales to look for my bike?"

"Sure," I replied, "after we have our own garage sale this week."

Several days later, we set up for our annual sale. This year, for the first time, we ran out of tables to hold the toys, games, and clothes we wanted to sell. When I saw my neighbor in her yard that night, I asked, "Kathleen, do you have a table we can borrow for our garage sale tomorrow?"

"I have a big, heavy one in the shed," she answered. "Can you help me move it?" Inside her darkened shed, I saw a large, round, wooden table and five bikes. She had two sons.

"Kathleen," I ventured, "you have a lot of bikes in here. Jonathan has outgrown his. If there's one your boys don't use anymore, could I buy it from you?"

After talking with her sons, she said, "You can have this white bike for free. The boys don't use it anymore. We don't even remember where we got it. All it needs is a new tire." She rolled the bike out of the shed and I took it home.

Jonathan was already asleep in bed, but I whispered in his ear, "God is already answering your prayer for a new bike."

Early the next morning, Jonathan rushed outside to see his new bike. He sat on it and grinned from ear to ear. "Thank you, Jesus," he chirped, "for a bike that's just my size!" *Lord, You are so good. Thanks for showing Your love to Jonathan!*

"Mom, what does *Schwinn* mean?" he asked after reading the bike label.

"It means God has given you a sturdy and dependable bike."

"Please can we go get the tire *now* so I can ride my new bike?" he pleaded.

"As soon as you get home from school today," I promised.

That afternoon we drove to three different stores. Each had lots of bike tires, but not the size we needed. *This is strange. What is so unusual about this tire?* Finally, we stopped at a bike shop. Thankfully, it had the right size tire. As I paid for it, I told the clerk, "We went to three other stores, but none had this tire. I'm sure glad you have it in stock."

"This tire is for a twenty-two-inch bike," he responded. "Schwinn doesn't make that size bike anymore."

*Father, You are full of surprises. You knew exactly what Jonathan meant when he prayed for a bike just his size. You gave him a good quality, perfect-sized bike that can no longer be purchased. I'm glad this bike needed a new tire. It showed Jonathan and me how specifically You answer our prayers.*

### *Follow the Leader*

*Father, thank You for providing for us through AFDC during the past six years so I could be home and nurture my children. Thank You for planting a deep commitment to them in my heart. Thanks for Your deep commitment to me.*

I traveled a different path than most of my peers: gladly staying home with my children. This route didn't fit some people's expectations. They applied subtle and not-so-subtle pressure, urging me to get a real job and not waste my talents at home. I felt isolated and misunderstood. *Raising my children in a godly home is a real job. It uses all my abilities and continually challenges me. I'm thankful for speaking opportunities and classes at ACTS that coincide with my family priorities rather than conflict with them. Why do I have to justify my actions? Why do other people think they know what's best for my life?*

I constantly sought God's guidance in making choices, yet often felt judged by others. *Father, You are my stability and security. My one desire is to please You. I don't like feeling defensive about my life or my decisions. Please give me a sentence or phrase so I can graciously respond when people keep asking about my future plans.*

I waited expectantly for God's answer. He was silent. I continued waiting for months. At a conference, a speaker's illustration caught my attention. "In the game 'Follow the Leader,' the object is to go where the leader goes and do what he does," he explained. "The leader doesn't walk in a straight line; he winds all over the place. Those at the front of the line follow him best."

"The Christian life is like playing 'Follow the Leader,'" he continued. "Jesus calls us to follow Him: to go where He goes, do what He does, and say what He says. Those closest to Him follow best. It's not important to know in advance where you are going. What *is* important is your present relationship with Him."

A light flashed on in my mind and a grin spread across my face. *I'm following Jesus! That's what my life is all about. I'm following Jesus! These puzzle pieces of my life that don't seem to connect are all part of following Him. It is like the game. It doesn't matter how my life looks to others. The key is staying very close to Jesus. Now I know what to tell others about my future: I'm following Jesus, and wherever He leads, I will follow.*

### Burdened by Debt

"Oh no, the washing machine isn't working again," I muttered. I checked the warranty papers and quickly called the repairman. *I'm glad he can fix it today. The warranty expires next week.* I was agitated by my awkward predicament with the washer and dryer—one that had burdened me for five years. I mentally rehashed my dilemma one more time.

The duplex we moved into in 1989 had laundry hookups, but no washer and dryer. My friend Bobbie told me, "Pick out a washer and dryer you like. You can pay me back when you're on your feet again."

I didn't want to go into debt. Moving had increased my rent and utilities $100 a month, but my income hadn't changed. *If possible, I'd much rather do our laundry at home than make endless trips to the laundromat with my three children.* With mixed feelings, I accepted Bobbie's offer. A trusted friend advised me on which appliances to buy. The total bill of $770 reinforced my initial fears. *That's more than my monthly income. How will I ever pay that debt?*

Several times that year I offered to pay a few dollars toward my debt, but each time Bobbie said, "Just wait until you're settled." After a while, I dropped the subject completely. *Every penny we have goes for basic family needs.*

Year after year my debt troubled me. *This debt is like dragging around a ball and chain.* I didn't ask God for help. I totally avoided talking to Him about it. I knew God didn't want me to be in debt. I felt embarrassed and ashamed. *I've gotten myself into this mess. I'll have to find my own way out of it.*

When 1994 began, my debt felt like a noose around my neck. *The five-year warranty on these appliances expires in June and I haven't paid a cent. There's no way out of this debt.* My income remained the same as in 1989: $621 a month from AFDC. Honorariums from speaking went directly to ACTS for tuition. They didn't increase my income for daily living.

In May I was thrilled to learn my rent would decrease by $113 per month. *Now we'll have more money for daily living expenses. I'm sure I can pay ten dollars every month toward the washer and dryer debt. But at that rate, it'll take six years to pay it off.*

Still pondering my plight, I led the repairman down to the washer that afternoon. *How could I have let this debt go unpaid all these years?*

"This is your fourth repair," the repairman said when he finished working. "You're eligible for a new washer."

"What do you mean?"

"According to your warranty, if you have more than three repairs in five years, the company will replace your machine."

"It's hard to believe they'd do that."

"Go check it out. Be sure to take your paperwork."

*The salesperson will probably laugh at me. But I'd better give it a try while the washer's still under warranty.* I drove to the appliance store and hesitantly approached the customer-service person. "My washer just had its fourth repair in five years," I timidly told him and handed him the warranty papers.

He checked his computer for several minutes. "That model isn't manufactured any longer," he announced, his eyes still on the computer screen.

"Oh," I groaned. *I feel like such a fool.* I slowly backed away from the counter. *Why did I come here?*

"We'll have to give you a better model, free of charge," he continued. "We can deliver it and pick up your old washer in three days."

*Father, I can hardly believe this. Your timing is marvelous. Just when I can start paying for the old appliances, You give me a brand new, improved washer.*

I called Bobbie to apologize for my delay in paying my debt, tell her my payment plan, and share God's provision of a new washer. As I talked with her, God carried on a totally different conversation with me.

"Linda," He said, "I provided both washers and the dryer for you. The debt itself is not the issue here. Your sin is your stubborn refusal to come to Me about this debt."

My $770 debt suddenly weighed a ton. I fell to my knees. *God, for five years I've avoided You about this debt. I thought I had to work it out alone. Please forgive me for leaving You out of my mess. I need You. Thank You for forgiving me because of Jesus. He paid for all my sins on the cross—even those with this washer and dryer debt. Please make a way for me to pay off this debt quickly. I want to be free from this burden. Thank You for what You will do.*

God spoke to me personally from His Word. "Call upon Me in the day of trouble; I shall rescue you, and you will honor Me" (Psalm 50:15, NASB). "Because he has loved Me, therefore I will deliver him; I will set him securely on high, because he has known My name. He will call upon Me, and I will answer him; I will be with him in trouble; I will rescue him and honor him"(Psalm 91:14-15, NASB). *Father, these are Your promises to rescue me. You will act on my behalf because of our relationship.*

"Linda," He said, "I know your heart in all of this. You are fully committed to Me. I am your rescuer and I will gladly rescue you." *Father, I know so little of Your rescuing love. Thank You for these lessons that reveal You to me.*

I told my children about the debt. We made it a family prayer project. We set aside a small box to hold money for paying the debt, and God began to rescue me. On walks with a friend, I frequently found pennies, nickels, or dimes in the street. A store advertised a swimsuit sale. I took back my receipt and got a $12.60 refund. A neighbor insisted on paying me five dollars for driving her children to school for her one day. I typed a student's term papers. She gave me forty dollars. I gave a friend several guitar lessons. At the last lesson, she surprised me with a fifty-dollar bill. In both cases, the money was an unexpected gift, since I'd volunteered for those tasks. Our reduced rent made more money available to put toward the debt. By mid August, I had paid $350 of the $770.

"God is providing for the washer and dryer," Jonathan observed, "just like He did for our trip to Grandma and Grandpa's."

In September, God provided in different ways. A friend bought school clothes for my children. Someone took me clothes shopping. Another friend gave Timothy some clothes. Money I would have spent on clothes for our family helped pay the debt instead. By September 30, I had paid $500. By October 31, I had paid back $650.

*Father, there's only $120 to go. I want to pay off this debt by Thanksgiving. Please help me.* An unexpected fifty dollars came in the mail. A friend gave me money to pay for my children's athletic fees. I paid the final seventy dollars of the debt from my regular income.

*Father, my heart overflows with joy this Thanksgiving. You have rescued me and removed this burden that was crushing me. The debt I couldn't repay in five years, once placed in Your hands, has been fully paid in six months. All things are possible with You, Lord. Now I'm totally debt free!*

### Constant Pain

"My head hurts all the time, Mom," ten-year-old Rachel moaned. "It never stops." Her forehead and the top of her head hurt, the area a baseball cap would cover. She hadn't fallen or hit her head. Rachel's headache persisted whether she sat up, stood, or laid down. *What's causing this horrible headache?*

We prayed every day and asked many people to pray for Rachel. After a week of constant pain, I took her to the pediatrician. He examined Rachel but had no definite answers. He prescribed medication, but it didn't ease her pain. Her headache continued through October and November with no relief. *If only I could do something. I feel so helpless. God, please heal Rachel.*

We read Bible verses about God's healing power. I took Rachel to a Healing Center for prayer. Her headache persisted. After waiting six painful weeks for an appointment, Rachel was examined by a pediatric neurologist. She ordered multiple tests for Rachel. All the test results came back normal. The doctors couldn't pinpoint any specific cause for her headache.

"God loves you, Rachel," I told her many times. "He knows what is causing your headache, even if the doctors don't. He is caring of you."

Rachel's eyes brimmed with tears. "My head hurts so much," she cried. "Why won't this headache go away?"

*I wish I had some answers. Help us, God.*

I developed a "headache scale" to help Rachel describe her pain. "One" meant minimal pain; "ten" meant excruciating pain. "My headache hurts more than a 'ten,'" Rachel cried.

*Oh God, please heal her. You are our only hope.*

A few weeks later, after an appointment with a Christian chiropractor, Rachel's headache slightly subsided. After her next visit, her headache lessened to a "seven" on the scale. Each day the pain decreased. Finally, on February 7, 1995, God healed Rachel. Her headache was totally gone! *Thank You, Father, for answering our prayers.*

We held a praise party with friends who had prayed for Rachel. After going out together for pizza, we returned home and sang our favorite praise songs to God. His sweet presence filled our living room and our hearts.

A few days after God healed Rachel, I asked her, "What did you learn about God through all of this? Let's try and write it down so you'll remember how God helped you through this hard time. Maybe someday you'll be able to encourage someone else who's hurting." Together, we wrote down her story.

News of Rachel's healing spread quickly. The following Sunday, she shared her testimony in church. "Four months seems like a world record headache," Rachel said with a knowing sigh. "God healed me of my horrible headache!" she exclaimed. "God will heal everyone who asks Him, but He doesn't always do it right away. Sometimes it takes a while. If you are sick, ask God to heal you. He will heal you in His time."

*Father, thank You for the faith You firmly rooted in Rachel's heart through this painful ordeal. Thank You for her testimony of Your goodness.*

### Connected

My reasons for attending ACTS were totally different than God's. I enrolled to study God's Word and sharpen my ministry skills. God brought me to ACTS to teach me about relationships in the Body of Christ. He worked through people to dissolve the insulation I had built around my heart to protect me from future hurt. I needed to learn to trust people again. I needed to experience being family in the Body of Christ.

I isolated myself from other students. God intervened. The school administrator asked me to welcome Pam, a new student, and show her around. In our first conversation, something clicked. We had much in common: our love for Jesus, children at home, being part-time students, and balancing school and other responsibilities. That morning I talked more with Pam than I'd talked with all the other students over several months. God began knitting our hearts together. We became companions on our journey through ACTS. *Thanks, Father, for the gift of Pam. She's that everyday kind of friend I prayed for long ago.*

Jim, another student, surprised me one morning. "Linda," he said, "since yesterday, God has been prompting me to say something to you. I want to ask your forgiveness on behalf of men, especially those who have hurt you."

My eyes filled with tears. I had specifically forgiven the men in my life who had hurt me, but my inner wounds were not fully healed. *Lord, please heal my heart and restore me to wholeness.*

Some days my responsibilities overwhelmed me. "I can't handle all this," I cried in my small group. "I've got three children to care for, school assignments, preparation for speaking at several churches, plus laundry, cooking, raking leaves, and putting in storm windows. I can't do it all."

Students prayed for me. Then Jim said, "I can come over this afternoon and rake your leaves." Betty volunteered to bring dinner. With Jim's help, my children and I raked up the leaves in record time. Betty took us all out for pizza. We joked and laughed for hours.

*Father, thanks for Jim and Betty. They're willing to give practical help and have fun with us.*

At ACTS, prayer became as natural as breathing. We learned to trust God to lead us in praying for each other. *Father, what were You doing in my heart just now as the students were praying for me? A picture came to my mind. I saw myself inside a small cell with cement walls and no windows. As I watched, Jesus walked down the hallway to my cell and unlocked the door with his key. Then He took me by the hand and led me out, saying, "Linda, I'm bringing you out of solitary confinement." I don't know how I got in there. I didn't even know I was in there. But this I know: Jesus is the One who brought me out!*

What did I learn during my three years at ACTS? In the Body of Christ, we're not just related; we're connected.

## Learning to Discern

New anxieties surfaced in my heart once 1995 began. *What will I do after graduation in June? I don't have a clue. What are Your plans for me, Father? I bring You all the unknowns, all the possibilities, all my responsibilities with my children, all my desires in serving You. I lay everything before You, Lord. I trust You to help me discern Your plans.*

While talking with my pastor in February, he said, "There's a possibility you could do a year-long internship here at the church once you graduate. Is that something you might be interested in?"

"I think so," I hesitated, taken by surprise.

"Well, you pray about it," he said. "We can talk more another time."

*Father, I fully entrust my future to You. Please reveal Your plans for me. I only want to follow as You lead.*

In March I had my annual re-certification interview for AFDC, food stamps, and Medical Assistance. Each year it stirred up conflicting emotions within me. *Father, I've experienced condescension and prejudice being on AFDC. A spirit of oppression seems to fill the entire welfare building. Please free me from the condemnation I feel after being there today.*

*Father, I'm grateful for Your provision through the welfare system. It has allowed me to stay home and raise my own children. You have also provided opportunities for me to earn money within welfare regulations: doing child care, working for the census, speaking, and leading Bible studies. You've supplied all my ACTS tuition through speaking. My car is paid for. I'm debt free. We live in a beautiful home. You are our provider, Father, and I trust you. In Your time, You will provide a way off this system that will not sacrifice my family priorities.*

In late March, my pastor and I discussed the possible internship. "It could be up to twenty hours a week," he said, "in areas tailored to your gifts and interests." *It sounds good, Father, yet I feel so uncertain.*

As graduation drew closer, my anxiety grew. *Father, I want concrete plans. I need to clearly hear from You. I only want to follow as You lead me.*

In early June, I received a phone call from a church thirty miles from my home. "You were highly recommended for a staff position," the pastor said. "Are you willing to meet me for an interview?"

I agreed. *Father, I don't want to close any doors You might be opening. Please give me Your discernment.*

"This position," the pastor explained, "involves overseeing all children's ministry: preschool, day care, Christian school, Sunday School, Vacation Bible School, outreaches, and special programs. It would start part-time and expand."

"What does part-time mean?" I asked, amazed by the scope of the job.

"Sunday mornings, Wednesday nights, and two other days; a flexible schedule."

"What about salary?"

"I can't give any range right now," he replied. "There is bartering. You could work in exchange for your children's tuition at our school." *Father, help me. This job would mean moving or a long commute. You know what's best for our family. Please lead me.*

That afternoon, a package I had requested weeks ago arrived in the mail. It contained resources for adult Bible studies, support groups, divorce recovery, and single parenting. As I looked over the materials, I started crying. *Father, I deeply desire to help adults cling to You and Your Word. I long to bring hope and healing to those shattered by divorce. I want to encourage those who have no hope.*

God used those materials to confirm His direction for me: teaching, training, and equipping adults. I turned down the children's ministry position.

The following week, I met with my pastor again. "I'm very interested in the internship," I said. "Since my children are home during the summer, it would work best to begin once school starts in the fall."

"That's fine," he replied. "We'll work out the details then."

I graduated from ACTS with great joy. God had given me the vision and perseverance to finish the AA in Ministerial Training degree in three years. *Thank You, Father, for Your daily grace to complete this degree.*

I plunged into a fun-filled summer with my children: camping, going to ball games, swimming at the city pool, and playing at parks. I anticipated serving God and His people through my upcoming internship. I had no inkling of the major change God would reveal to our family before the summer ended.

### Dreams Restored

"Mom, can you homeschool us?" Rachel asked one summer evening in 1995.

"Yeah, can you?" chimed in Timothy and Jonathan.

"God would have to work a miracle," I replied. "There's much more involved in homeschooling than you know."

I had first learned about homeschooling when Timothy was a toddler. It was the educational path I wanted to pursue with my children. But in 1988, when my husband and I separated, my dreams for homeschooling disintegrated. The responsibility of raising my three children alone crushed my hopes for homeschooling them.

I never told my children about my desire to homeschool. I didn't spend time thinking about it either. I knew in my life circumstances it would never happen. So I was totally surprised when my children, ages thirteen, ten, and eight, each began asking me to teach them at home. They talked about it all summer long. I kept putting them off. "You can pray about it." I said. "I'd love to have you home, but I don't see how it's possible."

They gave wonderful reasons for wanting to be taught at home, but from my perspective, our conversations were pointless. I knew many families that homeschooled, but I never discussed it with them. I did not know any single parents who homeschooled. Those words didn't fit together. I believed it was impossible for a single parent to homeschool.

One August afternoon at the city pool, Jonathan came running over to me. "Mom," he panted, "Joe is going to be homeschooled this year."

My ears perked up immediately. Joe's mom was single. "Is his mom here?" I asked.

"Yeah, she's right over there," he pointed. And off he ran to swim again.

I quickly sought her out. "Please tell me everything you've found out about homeschooling," I said. "How did you reach your decision? What are your plans?"

During our brief conversation, all my assumptions about homeschooling—that it was too complicated, that I couldn't work and homeschool, that it involved too much time and paperwork—were blown away. The possibility of homeschooling my children erupted within me. *Father, is this part of Your plan for us this year? Could I handle it? Could I provide what my children need and also fulfill my internship requirements? Please give me Your wisdom.*

The next day, Claire, a pioneering home educator in our city, showed me her curriculum materials and explained why she'd chosen them. "You don't have to spend a lot of money to homeschool," she said. "Many books in your home can be used. The public library is a great resource. Start with what you have."

Claire taught her children at home some years and sent them to public school other years. "Whatever seems best for that child and our family situation guides our decisions about homeschooling," she concluded. Her perspective encouraged me to make a decision for only this year.

A home educator from church advised, "If you can only homeschool one child, homeschool the oldest." That surprised me. I thought Timothy, entering eighth grade, was too old to teach at home.

Our church held its annual camping trip that weekend. I talked with every homeschooling family there. *Father, You know I want to invest deeply in my children's lives and shape their character. You have stirred up this desire in me to homeschool. But can I really handle it? I bring You all my fears, especially the fear of being overwhelmed.* As I kept praying, God spoke tenderly to me. "I will instruct you and teach you in the way you should go; I will counsel you and watch over you" (Psalm 32:8).

I didn't have months to think or pray about this. School would start in another week. I needed to make a decision now. I fervently prayed for God's direction and sensed Him urging me to take this step of faith. *Father, I entrust all the details to You. It seems best right now to home-school Timothy and Rachel and keep Jonathan in public school. Please give me the privilege of homeschooling him in the future. I'm trusting You to design a tailor-made course of study for us. Please let homeschooling and my internship complement one another, for You are clearly leading me into both areas.*

One week had passed since my conversation at the swimming pool. Now I launched into the whole new world of homeschooling. *It's all part of following Jesus.*

Claire helped me decipher the official forms required by our school district. Another friend loaned me her curriculum catalogs. "I'll bring your children to my house," she said. "Take whatever time you need to plan." My children spent most of three days at her home! *Thank You, Father, for this practical help from these homeschooling moms. I couldn't have gotten started without their support.*

Homeschooling and my internship fit together well. God had arranged my family priorities to take highest precedence. My internship supported that commitment.

While completing the initial paperwork, I learned that every homeschool must have a name. I wracked my brain and asked my children for ideas, but no names seemed right for us. Suddenly, "Abiding Hope" shot through my mind. God had revealed Himself as my Abiding Hope during my marriage crisis in 1989. Now those words took on new meaning. *Father, You are our hope, the center and focus of our school. We put our trust and confidence in You.* Abiding Hope Academy, our homeschool, is a testimony to God's faithfulness. He restored hopes and dreams He had planted in my heart years ago.

\* \* \*

1. What hope do these verses offer you right now: Jeremiah 29:11, Proverbs 3:5-6? How can they help you when your future seems uncertain?

2. Why is going into debt so easy? Why doesn't God want us to be in debt? What help does God offer to get us out of debt?

3. In what area of your life have you lost hope? What dream is God restoring in your life?

*Father, You are the God of hope. Anchor my hope in You.*

## Chapter Five

# God Is Trustworthy

*"O Sovereign LORD, you are God! Your*
*words are trustworthy"* (2 Samuel 7:28).

### Grandmas' Gifts

*It's 12:50 p.m. The truck will be here in ten minutes.* My
thoughts flashed back to a scene in Connecticut three
years earlier in August 1992.

Eight-year-old Rachel sat with her grandma at the
baby grand piano, taking her second "piano lesson" since
we arrived. "Curve your fingers like this," Grandma
demonstrated. "Always sit up straight and play with
expression. Now let me hear you play this part again."
Simple melodies flowed from the piano as Rachel played
her favorite songs for Grandma.

"I like playing your piano," Rachel told Grandma. "I
wish we had one at our house."

Later, Grandma told me, "Rachel's eager to learn and
catches on quickly. She reminds me of you when you
were little."

"Every day she plays the electric organ our friends gave us," I said. "I'm giving her lessons, but I'm amazed at what she teaches herself."

That fall, when I started classes at ACTS, Rachel's piano lessons gradually got pushed aside. *Rachel needs a piano teacher, but where can I find one? And how could I ever afford lessons for her?*

Grandma and Grandpa called one day in January 1993. "We think it would be good for Rachel to take more piano lessons," they said. "We'd like to help pay for them."

"That would be wonderful," I replied. Rachel and I immediately asked God to provide a piano teacher. Within weeks we found one. Rachel took lessons on her teacher's piano and practiced on our electric organ.

Rachel played songs over the telephone for Grandma. She made a cassette tape of her favorite songs and sent it to Grandma. *Thank You, Father, for providing this organ, the piano teacher, and the money for lessons. Thanks for Grandma's encouragement to Rachel in playing the piano.*

After months of lessons, Rachel grew frustrated with the organ. One keyboard didn't always have all the keys needed for a song and she had to play on both keyboards. "This is too confusing, Mom," she told me often. "Can we get a piano?"

"I've always wanted a piano," I admitted. *For more than twenty years I've wanted a piano, but we've never had money for one. I doubt we'll ever be able to afford one.*

In 1994, God provided money for airline tickets to visit Grandma and Grandpa. Several "piano lessons" with Grandma refueled Rachel's desire for a piano. "Mom, can we please get a piano?" she pleaded. "I like playing the piano much better than the organ."

"We'd have to sell the organ first," I said, trying to dampen her spirits. "There's not room in our house for both."

"Let's do that, Mom!" she exclaimed. "Then I could play our piano every day."

*I don't see how God could do it, but we can pray.* Every time Rachel asked about a piano, we prayed together. We prayed for a whole year. We found an upright piano, but it was too large for our living room. We advertised our organ at our garage sale, but it didn't sell. *Father, we are trusting You. Show us what to do.*

One day in September 1995, Rachel's dad said, "Rachel mentioned you want to sell your electric organ and get a piano. My mom wants to get an organ and take lessons. She might be willing to trade her piano for your organ."

*Father, is it possible that this might be Your plan?* My children visited their dad's relatives for birthdays and holidays, but I'd had little contact with them since the divorce. *If this is Your plan, Father, please work it out in a way that suits all of us.*

Rachel's grandma came to see our organ. "I'm looking for an organ like yours," she said. "My piano was given to me when my children were small, but I rarely play it now."

Rachel's piano teacher drove with me to examine the piano. "It's in very good condition," she said. "All it needs is a good tuning."

After praying for several days, I sensed God leading us to make the trade. Some of my friends moved the organ to Grandma's house. I contacted the piano moving company.

The clock struck one as the white truck pulled up in front of our house. We watched the movers carefully bring our new piano into the living room. *Father, this piano is a gift from You. Thank You for Rachel's joy in playing the piano, and her grandma's willingness to give it to us. Thank You that our electric organ is just what Rachel's grandma needs.* After the movers left, Rachel and I prayed over the piano. "Father, this is Your piano," we agreed. "We dedicate it to You for Your praise and glory." *Thank You, Father, for teaching us to bring our needs and desires to You. You've answered our prayers in ways I never could have imagined. Thank You for the precious gifts from each of Rachel's grandmas.*

### A Time to Trust

Our car died suddenly on the highway one Thursday night in October 1995. *I've always been fearful of car trouble with my children in the car. Now we're stranded. I'm not even sure where we are.* Rachel, Jonathan, and I left the car and began walking in the dark toward the last exit. "See those bright lights up there?" I asked my children. "Let's walk toward them." We scrambled up a steep grassy hill to a huge parking lot and fitness club. I frantically called Wes from the phone booth inside.

For three-and-a-half years, Wes had repaired our white Dodge Aries. He wasn't home that night, but his wife Gretchen was. She called their son. He borrowed a tow truck and came for us. *Thank You, Father, for providing people to help us.*

Wes called late that night. "The car may need a new engine," he said. "I'll be in North Dakota this weekend, so I can't get at your car until Monday."

During that weekend of waiting my mind became a breeding ground for fear. *What's wrong with our car? What will it cost to fix it? How will I ever pay the bill? I know our Promised Land Motors fund can't cover major repair like this.*

*Why isn't Wes here when I need him?* I knew it wasn't Wes's fault that he was out of town, but I still blamed him. I knew he had other commitments and car repair was not his profession, but I still felt abandoned. *Father, I've never had this kind of car crisis. Help me trust You. Please diagnose the problem and provide the parts and manpower needed.*

To fight my discouragement, I wrote a detailed record of how God had already cared for us in this situation:

> *The car died near an entrance ramp, not on a desolate part of the highway.*
>
> *Gretchen was home and called her son to help us. He was able to borrow a tow truck for our car, and he drove us home.*
>
> *Gretchen called Kristen and Phil. They picked up Timothy after his evening class so he wasn't stranded.*

I read through my list and thanked God for each detail of His care. *Father, please bless each person who helped us.*

On Monday afternoon, Kristen loaned me her car to run errands. When I returned it, her husband Phil asked, "What happened with your car?"

"Wes has been out of town," I explained. "He's looking over the car today. He said it might need a new engine."

When Phil learned that Wes was not a mechanic by trade, he said, "Call me if you need advice or help with the car." Only then did I realize Phil was a mechanic. I knew Kristen well, but had only met Phil once before.

The answering machine at home played a message from Wes. "Your car needs a new engine. I've called around but haven't found one yet. This could be pretty costly." His voice had never sounded so discouraged. I started crying. *Father, I feel so helpless. Why is this hap-*

*pening? This repair is far beyond Wes, his tools, and his capabilities. I desperately need You.*

I immediately called Phil with the news. "Have Wes call me," he replied. "Once I have specific information on the engine, I'm willing to look for one and possibly do the labor." *Father, thanks for bringing Phil into this situation. Your faithful provision so far encourages me to trust You for all that is still needed.*

On Tuesday morning, I rode with a co-worker to my internship at church. I shared my situation with the church staff. We prayed together and committed my needs to God. Another co-worker made arrangements so I could borrow her car for a few days. *Thank You, Father.*

I didn't hear from Wes that day or the next. *Why doesn't he call me? What's taking so long? Father, I'm leaning too heavily on Wes to fix our car. Please help me trust You.*

Wes called early Thursday morning. "Phil found an engine," he said, sounding relieved. "He'll tow your car and repair it over the weekend. The cost for the engine and parts is $550. You'll need to give him a check tomorrow. He won't charge you for labor. That's a tremendous blessing, but I know this is still a big expense."

In our church staff prayer time that morning, we rejoiced over God's provision. Together we asked Him to supply the needed money.

By evening I was frantic. *How can I possibly pay $550 by tomorrow? That's nearly a whole month's income.* I walked into my room, closed the door, and got down on my knees. *Father, I'm going to meditate on impossible situations in Your Word and how You came through. Please speak to me clearly as I seek You.* 2 Kings 4:1-7 came to mind. I quickly looked it up. *That's when God miraculously provided the oil to pay the* *widow's debts.* Elisha's question to the widow, "What do you have in your house?" jumped out at me.

I took out all my different budgeting envelopes with money for clothes, school, and upcoming expenses. I counted $449. *I didn't think I had that much money in these envelopes.* My checking account balance was $300. *I do have enough money here to pay for the engine. But Father, this money has to last us all month. What about the things this money is supposed to pay for? My children still need boots, mittens, and winter jackets.*

I poured out my heart to God. Gradually, my struggle changed to surrender. *Father, I will use the money You have provided to pay this bill. I will trust You for all our other needs.* An hour earlier, I'd been inconsolable. Now peace permeated my heart.

Fifteen minutes later, my pastor called. "Linda, I just returned from my trip and heard you had car trouble. What's the expense and what are you able to pay?"

After explaining my situation, I said, "Using the money at home and in checking, I can pay the bill."

"The church will pay half," he responded.

I couldn't believe my ears. "But I do have the money," I repeated.

"We want to bless you. Just stop by the church tomorrow and pick up the check."

"Thank you so much," I replied gratefully. *Father, You are so good. You change my heart so I'm willing to spend almost all our money on this bill and trust You for our needs. Then You intervene and bless us with this gift.*

I called Wes and Gretchen to share God's miraculous provision. As we praised God together over the phone, I realized it was exactly one week since I had first called

Wes for help. *Father, these days of worry felt more like weeks. Thank You for carrying me through this tough time.*

By Sunday evening, my car was fully repaired and home again. *Father, prosper Phil for helping us. Bless him abundantly for doing the labor free of charge. Father, thank You for these difficult car lessons. Thanks for the numerous ways You've demonstrated Your faithfulness. Help me trust You completely in every area of my life.*

### A Thankful Heart

"He who offers a sacrifice of thanksgiving honors Me" (Psalm 50:23, NASB). I meditated on this verse as 1996 began. *Father, I want to honor You. Forgive me for being quick to complain. Forgive me for sinking in self-pity instead of giving thanks for all You've done for me. Rather than endure this season of my life, I want to overflow with gratefulness.*

*Right now I give You thanks for these eight years of single parenting. Thank You for Your presence, Your comfort, and Your tender care each day. Thank You for taking a rotten situation and bringing incredible good out of it. Thank You for the ways You've changed me. My loneliness has led me to deeper intimacy with You. Being single has anchored my security in You. Please give me a thankful heart that sees You in every situation.*

*Father, I place this entire year of 1996 into Your hands. Each moment of each day, I want to be where You want me to be, do what You want me to do, and say what You want me to say. I totally abandon myself to You.*

*Father, please revolutionize my prayer life this year. Teach me how to pray about everything. I want to pray like I've never prayed before. I lift up Mom and Dad's fiftieth wedding anniversary coming in June. My children and I want to go, yet the cost of airline tickets is far beyond our budget. Please make a way for us. I'm trusting You.*

*Thank You for going ahead of me into 1996. There are no surprises for You, Lord. Thanks for all You will do in my life this year.*

### Perfect Timing

After seventeen years of constant use, our hideaway bed couch felt lumpy to sit on or sleep on. When I received gift money last December, I set aside $100 toward a new couch. More gift money provided a total of $400. *Lord, we definitely need a dependable hideaway bed for my parents' visits. Please give me Your wisdom about getting one.*

I shopped around and fretted for days about spending that money. Finally, I convinced myself to buy one. I hurried back to the store before its sale ended.

"We're out of stock in that design," the salesman informed me, "but you can order it today at the sale price and have your new couch in about three weeks."

"That sounds great to me," I replied. "What's your store rebate policy?"

"If this hideaway bed goes on sale within thirty days of purchase, you can get it for that sale price. For you, that starts now through thirty days after your couch is delivered."

"What a deal! I'm sure I'll get a rebate on this," I said.

Two weeks later, on a Friday evening, an inner-city ministry picked up our old hideaway bed. Our new couch was scheduled to arrive within a week. We eagerly waited for the phone call from the furniture store.

The following Tuesday, our car quit running two different times during the day. *How can this be? It just got a new engine last October.* I called Wes. The first day he could work on it was Friday. *Father, thanks for Wes. Thanks for holding us in the palm of Your hand.*

On Thursday morning, our family discussed the Bible story of Jesus feeding 5,000 people (John 6:1-15). "Jesus had resources His disciples knew nothing about," I told my children. That sentence flashed like a neon sign inside my head. When we finished talking and praying, I went to my room to be alone with God. *Father, Your unlimited resources extend far beyond my ability to provide. We have car problems. We also need money for flying to Mom and Dad's fiftieth anniversary party in June. Please increase my confidence in You. Whatever it takes, I want to be deeply trusting, not anxious or fearful.*

That afternoon the furniture store called. "Your couch arrived today," the salesman said. "Once you make your final payment we'll deliver it."

"I'll be there tomorrow," I assured him, "as soon as my car is repaired."

Late that night, Wes called. "Linda, I have good news and bad news. Which do you want first?"

"I'll take the good news."

"The good news is Jesus loves you very much. The bad news is your car needs major repair. It'll cost about $400. I've arranged for Phil to do the work. You'll be without a car for five days." In my mind I saw all our couch money sprout wings and fly away. *Now we'll never be able to buy that couch.*

When I didn't respond, Wes spoke again. "God is teaching you about persevering trust, Linda. Consider the $400 as tuition for this class in the School of the Spirit. The outcome in your life will far outweigh the cost."

His words reminded me of God's Word that morning. *Jesus, You have resources I know nothing about. Help me trust You.*

Five days later I picked up my car. Actual repairs cost $346. *That's less than the estimate, but I had to use the couch money to pay the bill. Now we'll never be able to pay for that couch.* In the morning, I saw my situation from a different perspective. *Father, You provided that money and met our immediate need for car repair. Your timing was perfect. You are dependable and faithful. Now please help me trust You for our couch.*

"Can you hold that couch until I'm able to pay for it?" I anxiously asked the furniture salesman. "I just had an urgent car repair."

"If someone else wants to buy it before then" he replied, "we'll have to sell it to them." *Father, please watch over our couch. I'm trusting You.*

"I'm so anxious about money," I told Gretchen two weeks later. "Our couch money paid for car repairs. It'll take forever for me to save up that amount. I'm wondering if I should use up my savings account to pay for the couch. But I always thought my savings was only for emergencies. A couch isn't an emergency."

"Who knows," she replied, "maybe God had you save that money for this specific need."

Her words stuck in my mind all evening. Late that night, I knelt by my bed and prayed. *Father, forgive me for clinging to my savings account. You are my security, not that money. Forgive me for doubting Your faithfulness when You demonstrate it repeatedly. Forgive me for thinking I'd used up Your allotment of help and You'd left me to my own resources. Father, please develop in me a supernatural trust in You that cannot be shaken.*

I emptied my savings account and made the final couch payment. Our hideaway bed was delivered three weeks after the car repairs. *Thank You, Father.*

During my quiet time the next day, God led me to Jeremiah 17:7-8 (NASB):

*"Blessed is the man who trusts in the* LORD *And whose trust is the* LORD. *For he will be like a tree planted by the water, That extends its roots by a stream And will not fear when the heat comes; But its leaves will be green, And it will not be anxious in a year of drought Nor cease to yield fruit."*

*Father, those promises gave me hope during my separation. Now, eight years later, I sense You're giving them to me for my whole life. Please make me a living example of one fully dependent on You.*

Two days later, I found a plain white envelope in my mailbox at church. As I picked it up, God whispered, "I am the same, five minutes before you open this envelope, right now, and five minutes from now. I do not change." It held $200 in gift certificates to a grocery store!

*Thank You, Father. You are always faithful. My thankfulness must be based on Your character, not Your provision.*

Two weeks later, while glancing through the Sunday paper, I exclaimed, "Look! That's our couch on the front-page ad!"

"Where?" my children asked. "Let me see!"

"The price listed is less than we paid," I explained. "We've had our couch less than thirty days, so they have to refund the difference." I took my receipt to the store and got $100 back.

*Father, You are so creative. Your timing amazes me. Money You provided paid for car repairs instead of the couch. After I used my savings account to buy the couch, You provided $200 for groceries. The delay in getting the couch gave me back $100 today. You do have unlimited resources. You have faithfully met all our needs.*

## An Enormous Family

Severe stomach cramps and excruciating back pain woke me in the middle of the night. I tossed and turned for hours. *I think I need to see a doctor. I'll ask Kristen to take me when she comes today for our weekly 6 a.m. prayer meeting.*

At 5:30 a.m. my phone rang. "I'm not coming over," Kristen said. "There's been a huge snowstorm during the night."

"I'm really sick," I said, describing my symptoms. "If I'm not feeling better later on, could you take me to the doctor?"

"Just give me a call," she replied. "I have the day off."

I called her back at 7:30 a.m. "Kristen, I need your help," I moaned. She shoveled through a snowdrift in her driveway, then drove to my house. She helped me walk to her van and drove me to the emergency room. Doubled over in pain, I felt like I was dying. Kristen stayed with me through six painful hours of tests.

"This is a gallstone attack," the doctor concluded. "It's unusual for you to be in such pain. Here's a prescription. We've set up an appointment for you with your doctor tomorrow. He'll schedule your surgery. You can go home now."

*Why can't they take my gallbladder out now? Father, please arrange my surgery for the best possible time.*

On Tuesday, my doctor ordered more tests. He scheduled my surgery for Wednesday, April 3, more than a week away. *This pain is unbearable. How will I care for my children? I can't even sit up.*

Gretchen called me that night. "Linda, I'm taking tomorrow off from work and will come over for the day. I'll help Timothy and Rachel do the laundry, wash the dishes, clean the house, and deliver their paper routes.

*Father, thanks for answers to prayers I don't have the strength to pray.*

All day Wednesday stomach cramps and stabbing back pain continued. That night, I called people to care for my children during surgery. My doctor called to check on me. "You shouldn't be in such pain," he cautioned. "If you're not feeling better by morning, come back in."

*Thank You, Father, for my doctor's care.*

After a pain-filled, sleepless night, I returned to the clinic for more tests. "We'll try to reschedule surgery earlier next week," the doctor said. "A nurse will call you at home later today."

*Father, I'm afraid. Please take this pain away. I've never been so sick in my life. Please care for my children.*

At 5 p.m. the nurse called. "Your surgery has been moved up to Monday afternoon. You'll need to see the surgeon tomorrow."

"But I just saw my doctor today," I moaned.

"The surgeon wants to see you in the morning."

That evening I contacted people to care for my children on the new surgery date. Others agreed to deliver my children's Wednesday paper routes. *People are so willing to help us. Father, I feel cared for in each phone conversation, in each prayer prayed for me.*

On Friday I couldn't keep any food down. The surgeon saw me briefly, and then told the nurse, "Let's get this scheduled for tomorrow." A few minutes later he told me, "Your surgery is set for 9:30 tomorrow morning."

"What time do I have to be at the hospital?" I asked. "I don't have any family in the area."

"Be there by 7:30 a.m.," he replied.

*It's already noon. I have to arrange my ride to the hospital and find families for my children to stay with tonight and this weekend. This constant pain is unbearable. Father, please give me the strength I need right now.*

I called Gretchen as soon as I got home. *She's not leaving town until Monday. Maybe she can drive me and stay with me tomorrow.*

After I explained the surgery date change, she responded, "Linda, I can take you. I want to be with you and pray for you during surgery."

*Thank you, Jesus.*

Two families agreed to take my children overnight. A friend promised to take them to an Easter drama we had planned to attend with her on Saturday. Another offered to keep them overnight after the drama and bring them to church on Sunday. My children would spend Sunday afternoon with their father, and he'd take them to the families they'd stay with during the week.

By 5 p.m. my children were packed for the week and picked up by other families. Exhausted and in severe pain, I collapsed on the couch. *Father, You've worked out every detail. Thanks for providing all the help I've needed this week, and for those who will help during surgery and recovery. You are faithful. I feel so loved and cared for.*

Suddenly, I remembered the words I'd spoken to the surgeon that morning. *Father, forgive me for saying "I have no family in the area." That's an absolute lie. Here's the truth: I have an enormous family in Jesus that loves me and would do anything they can to help me.* Tears ran down my cheeks as I recalled all the people who had generously given their time and resources to care for us. *Thank You, Father, for each person. So many people are praying for us.*

Gretchen drove me to the hospital in the morning. During admission procedures, the registrar asked for my "next of kin." *All my relatives are out of state.* Then I remembered what God had revealed to me the night before. I glanced at Gretchen, smiled, and gave her name. *Gretchen, my "next of kin"—I like that.*

After surgery, two beautiful roses with a card signed "next of kin" brightened my room. "The doctor gave me the full report," my "next of kin" told me. "Your surgery went very well."

*Thank you, Father, for changing my surgery date so Gretchen could be with me. I feel deeply loved and cared for.*

A family from church drove me home on Sunday. Betty, a friend from ACTS, stayed with me overnight. We laughed a lot, even though it hurt my incisions. Everything seemed funny after the constant pain of the previous week. When I settled into bed that night, Betty knelt down and prayed for me.

After work on Monday, Betty ran errands for me, brought us Chinese food for dinner, and gave me a manicure. "I can also stay over tomorrow night," she said, "and I don't work on Wednesday. So I can do your laundry, cleaning, and vacuuming then."

*Thank You for Betty, Father. Through her kindness I've experienced Your gentle love.* Others stopped by with meals during the week. One friend loaned me several of her favorite books. Another brought Rachel and Jonathan to visit me briefly.

*Father, this week of recovery is a gift from You. My children are well cared for, and so am I. Your presence here is so gentle and real. I feel wrapped up in Your love. Thank You for each person who has touched us with Your love and comfort during these two weeks. I do have an enormous family.*

## One Thing

Any time I had car problems, I called Wes. Knowing he would help gave me great peace of mind.

Eight months after setting up Promised Land Motors, Wes came to me and said, "Linda, your car debt of $500 is canceled...our gift to you. The little white car is fully yours."

*That's a big debt to cancel. Why would he do that? And what about AFDC? Will I lose my grant now?*

As if reading my mind, Wes continued, "Let me know when the car has decreased enough in value that it won't affect your AFDC grant. Then I'll sign it over to you."

I was speechless. *Why would he do this for me?*

Wes replaced the car battery late one night when it was twenty degrees below zero. Another time while repairing the car, he accidentally grabbed one of his car keys instead of mine and put it into my car ignition. It got stuck. Wes had to take the entire steering mechanism apart to fix it. *That'll be the last time he ever repairs this car. Promised Land Motors just went down the drain.* But Wes kept fixing my car.

One day the radiator quit working. A service station wanted to make extensive repairs. I called Wes for advice. "I'll tow the car to my house and repair it," he said. Within an hour, he was working on my car in his driveway. I learned then that he was leaving the next day for a month-long mission trip to the Ukraine.

*I am such a disturbance in his life. Why is he helping me? How can he take time today to fix this car?* When Wes realized he couldn't finish the repairs that day, he arranged for his son to complete the work.

When the car needed a new engine, I was totally convinced Wes would never ever have anything to do with that car again. *Promised Land Motors is over for sure this time.* But Wes kept fixing my car. He never showed any frustration or resentment when he worked on it. He simply smiled and said, "It's all part of the service." *Why does he keep fixing my car? What's in this for him?*

Finally, after he had cheerfully repaired my car for more than four years, I got up the courage to talk to him about it. "Wes," I said, "I don't understand why you keep fixing my car."

"Linda," he replied, "when you were in so much pain from your divorce I asked God how I could help you. He said, 'Be faithful in *one* thing.' When I had the chance to lease this car to you and maintain it, I knew this could be my 'one thing.'"

"But you don't get upset with me when it's not working. And even when you have other things to do, you don't tell me to stop calling you."

"When I promised to take care of your car, Linda, I knew it would need to be serviced. God told me this would be a practical way to be a support to you. I'm committed to helping you in this way. It's that simple."

*Father, through Wes's care for our car, I've felt Your care. Please pour out Your abundant blessing on him. His faithfulness in this "one thing" has demonstrated Your faithfulness to me.*

\* \* \*

1. How can God use recurring problems (in health, finances, car repair, relationships, etc.) to draw us closer to Himself? Give an example from your life. How has God shown His trustworthiness to you in the midst of your struggles?

2. 1 Peter 5:7 says, "Cast all your anxiety on him because he cares for you." The word *cast* is a fishing term meaning "to throw upon." What problem are you facing, either large or small, that you have not yet cast on God?

3. Who has demonstrated God's faithfulness to you? How have they done it? Consider telling them how they've touched your life.

*Father, You are trustworthy. Please increase my trust in You.*

## Chapter Six

# God Is My Refuge

*The eternal God is your refuge
and underneath are the everlasting arms*
(Deuteronomy 33:27).

### *Breakthrough*

I'd never driven alone with my children on a trip over three hours from home. Fear of car trouble on the highway terrified me. But when my dear friend Pam moved 500 miles away, I resolved to overcome my fear. What started as a simple trip to see my friend turned into an all-out war against a longtime enemy.

My children and I eagerly prepared for our trip, but Fear eroded my enthusiasm. "You can't afford to go," Fear chided. "You barely have money for gas. How will you pay for repairs when your car breaks down?"

*Father, please protect our car.*

"You'll probably fall asleep at the wheel and crash," Fear harassed.

*I wonder if we should go at all. We still don't have enough money to fly to Connecticut for my parents' anniversary in June. Maybe I should forget about this trip and put the money toward our plane tickets. Help me, God. I don't know what to do. What are Your plans for us?*

Fear laughed as confusion clouded my thinking.

"I want you to take both trips," God answered. "I have different purposes for each one." His clear answer calmed my heart, at least for the moment.

The day before our departure, I called Pam. "I'm afraid to drive on this trip," I stammered. "I'm afraid the car will break down or I'll fall asleep at the wheel. I know God wants me to overcome my fear, but it's paralyzing me. Please pray for me."

Pam had driven many long trips alone. This wasn't a battleground for her. Yet she listened compassionately. "I'll pray for you right now and as you travel," she reassured me. I felt strengthened and encouraged as she prayed with me about every detail of the trip.

Another friend gave me a Bible verse for the trip:

*"Do not fear, for I am with you; Do not anxiously look about you, for I am your God. I will strengthen you, surely I will help you, Surely I will uphold you with My righteous right hand"* (Isaiah 41:10, NASB).

*You are my faithful God. You're helping me face my fears. Thanks for all You will do in me on this trip.*

The next day we packed the car, headed west, and drove for hours. About fifty miles from our motel, the car's power-loss light suddenly flashed on. "The last time this happened," Fear hissed, "your car died on the highway and needed a new engine."

*Help, Father, I'm trusting You.*

"It's getting dark," Fear taunted. "You'll end up stranded by the side of the highway."

I prayed with my children for God's protection and kept driving. Each time I looked down and saw that red power-loss light, I chose to keep my eyes on Jesus. *Please God, help me not to panic.* As we turned off the highway to our motel, the power-loss light shut off. *What's wrong with our car, Lord? What should I do?*

While my children swam in the motel pool, I meditated on the Bible verse I'd been given for the trip. *Father, Your Word gives the reason not to fear: You are with me! I'd rather have You here with me than anyone else. Please anchor this truth in my heart: I am not alone.*

Early the next morning, I studied those verses again. *Father, You give me three specific promises:* "I will strengthen you." *You did last night when I felt sleepy while driving.* "Surely I will help you." *You helped me stay calm when the power-loss light turned on.* "Surely I will uphold you with My righteous right hand." *Father, You are carrying me on this journey. I give You all my anxieties about the car. No matter what happens, You are with me and I am safe.*

Soon after we re-entered the highway, the power-loss light flashed on again. The car didn't drive any differently, so I kept going. "You'll get stuck out here in the middle of nowhere," Fear harassed. "You were a fool to take this trip."

*Father, help me.*

Late that afternoon we arrived at Pam's house. I breathed a huge sigh of relief as I turned off the car. *Father, thanks for getting us here safely.* Our fun-filled weekend with Pam and her family flew by.

"You shouldn't have any car problems on your trip

home," a mechanic assured me. But as my family prepared to leave Pam's house, Fear gripped me again.

"Wait until you're back out on the highway," Fear threatened. "Then you'll find out what's really wrong with your car."

Pam and I prayed together. "Father, I commit our entire trip home to You," I cried as Fear shouted more lies in my ears.

"Thank You, Father," Pam prayed, "that You have planned ahead and made all the necessary arrangements for this trip. Please protect Linda, her children, and the car as they travel."

Fifteen miles down the highway, the power-loss light came on. Fear attacked, but this time I was prepared for battle. *God is with me. He is my strength. He is my helper. I am not alone.* Each time I glanced at the power-loss light, I pictured Jesus in the front seat with me. I recited God's promises. I sang praise songs. I used God's Word to destroy the lies that bombarded my mind. *You are with me, God. Your presence fills our car. That power-loss light is driving me deeper into Your embrace.*

We arrived home safely that night after eleven hours of travel. *Father, thank You for Your protection. Thanks for revealing that You are right here with me each time I drive my car. Whether the car drives safely or breaks down, You are always with me. You are the God of breakthrough. Thank You for my personal victory over Fear.*

## A Time for Honor

My parents' fiftieth wedding anniversary would be June 30, 1996. Being with them would honor them and their lifetime commitment to each other. When 1996 began, round-trip flights to Connecticut cost $500 per person. "Father, help us get the lowest fares possible," we had prayed as a family in January, "and please provide the money for our tickets."

*Father, I choose to rejoice in Your provision for this trip. Please change my thinking from "how will we ever have enough money for these plane tickets" to "thank You that You will provide exactly what we need for this trip."*

My gallbladder attack and surgery in late March had depleted my energy. I could only cope with one day at a time. One afternoon in April, I suddenly realized my parents' anniversary was only ten weeks away! *Father, I give You all my fears about money for this trip. I'm trusting You to make a way for us, just like You did for the Israelites so they could cross the Red Sea. You've provided fully in the past. Please work Your miracle for us now.*

Airline price wars lowered ticket costs to $283 each. *Help, Lord. We only have a total of $269.* Then I heard of tickets for $238 each. *Prices won't go lower than that, Father, but I'm already out of money for April. How will I ever be able to pay for airline tickets?*

God brought Psalm 50:23 (NASB) to my mind. "He who offers a sacrifice of thanksgiving honors Me; And to him who orders his way aright I shall show the salvation of God." I knew that being with my parents for their anniversary would honor them. Now God showed me that thanking Him before I saw His provision would honor Him. *Father, I will honor You with my sacrifice of thanksgiving. I don't have the money for this trip, but You have unlimited resources. Thank You in advance for Your complete provision for every financial need on this trip: plane tickets, car rental, gifts, food, and activities.*

My mom called in early May. "The best fare our ticket agent can get at this time is $275 each," she said.

"Please have her reserve seats for us," I replied, giving my credit card information. *We don't have that much money, Father. Please help us.*

God worked on our behalf during the next several weeks. Friends donated items for our annual garage sale. We also sold cookies, brownies, and pop to raise money. Those sales brought our total trip savings to $344. I received twenty-five dollars for a market research test. My children contributed bonus money from their paper routes. A woman I'd never met handed me twenty dollars at a conference. These "surprises," plus money left from our trip to Pam's, went toward airfare.

Constant financial pressures burdened me. *Father, I don't have the money for this trip. In June my rent will increase twenty dollars a month. How am I supposed to support my family?* God reminded me of a verse I'd clung to during my first years as a single mom. "For the eyes of the LORD move to and fro throughout the earth that He may strongly support those whose heart is completely His" (2 Chronicles 16:9, NASB). *Father, I thought that verse meant You'd bring me through my immediate crisis of separation and divorce. Now I sense You are promising to strongly support me throughout my life as I walk according to Your plans. Father, I yield totally to You. Take me deeper in trusting You as my provider and provision.*

With careful budgeting and God's unusual provisions, we saved $758 by the end of May. But we still needed $308. Our tickets had to be paid for that week. *God, please show Yourself strong for us. Thanks for what You're doing that I can't see.*

I met my friend Gail for lunch on my birthday. "God has been providing for our trip in amazing ways," I rejoiced, and I shared His answers to our prayers.

"I want to give you a gift for your birthday and maybe toward your trip too, but I don't have my checkbook with me," she said. "You'll hear from me next week."

With our ticket money due in a few days, I was tempted to look to Gail to meet our need. As I left the restaurant, God distinctly said, "Don't trust Gail for your provision. I alone am your provision. Trust completely in Me, not in people."

Later that day, God spoke again. "Use your June AFDC check to pay the remaining ticket expense." *But God, what about our regular bills?* "I'll take care of you." *But the amount needed is nearly half of my AFDC check.* "I'll take care of you."

This was by far the biggest financial step of faith I had ever taken. When I wrote out the check for our tickets, I felt like I was jumping off the edge of a cliff. *Father, You alone are my provision. You are stretching me to trust You more.*

Financial pressures escalated during June. I struggled to pay for basic needs, like summer clothes for my children and toilet paper. There was no money to spare, yet each need was met, every bill paid on time. *Father, You are teaching me to trust You for each item we need. I'm also trusting You for the money we'll need during our trip. Thanks for the ten dollars I found on the floor at the store today. You are faithful day by day.*

On June 24, three days before our trip, I had eleven dollars left for the rest of the month. I had no savings. I had no other money. I would not get another AFDC check until we flew home after my parents' anniversary.

However, God had changed my heart during the previous weeks. Now I had a confidence in His faithfulness that could not be shaken. *Father, You are our provision. You provide in Your time. You are able to meet all our needs, even if we travel to Connecticut with only eleven dollars. Thank You for how You will provide for us.*

That afternoon I received a letter in the mail. "Sorry it's taken me so long to write," Gail said. "Use this gift for your birthday and your trip." Enclosed was a check for $500!

*Father, thank You for Your wonderful provision and for Gail.*

"Tithe from that gift," God said, "to show that you trust Me, not the money, as your provider."

Tears of joy filled my eyes as I gave fifty dollars to a family in desperate need. "God will provide for you as He has done for me," I encouraged as I hugged them. I set aside $100 as birthday money. The remaining $350 was "trip money" and meant to be spent.

My parents' fiftieth anniversary party was a joyous celebration with family and friends. All their children and grandchildren, gathered from across the country, sang "Great is Thy Faithfulness." *There is no one like You, Father. No one so dependable or trustworthy. You keep Your promises. You meet all our needs.*

After the party, my children and I stayed an extra week with my parents. With our "trip money" we rented a car, took them on an overnight trip, went sightseeing together, and spent a day at the ocean. We paid for meals and treated them twice at the homemade ice cream shop. *Father, You have provided abundantly. Thank You for the money to come here and bless my parents. Thank You for this opportunity to honor You. Thank You for this testimony of Your faithfulness.*

## Deliverance

"We need to talk," God said, shortly after we returned from my parents' celebration. I knew exactly what He was referring to. Some of my actions during the last two months embarrassed me. I replayed the whole scenario in my mind.

In the spring, while preparing for our trip to Pam's, God prompted me to bless Pam and Randy with thirty dollars. I set that money aside for them. Several times during our weekend at their home, I started to give them the money, but couldn't make myself do it. *What if I have car problems on our way home? I need this money right now. Once we're safely home, I can send them the money with a thank-you note.*

The irony of my situation was that the day before our trip a friend had given me thirty dollars to help cover expenses. I had missed God's message that came with the money: "I'm taking care of you, Linda."

After driving back home, I wrote to Pam and Randy and thanked them for welcoming us into their hearts and home. I didn't send a check. *We still need hundreds of dollars for our plane tickets. I'll put that thirty dollars toward airfare. I can send them twenty dollars for their twentieth anniversary in June.* Specific bills were due when I sent them their anniversary card. *I must pay these bills first. There's no extra money right now. I can always send it to them later.*

During our week with my parents, I read George Mueller's autobiography. He totally relied on God to supply all the needs of his family and thousands of orphans for over sixty years. He warned against hoarding what God provided. *I'm hoarding that thirty dollars, thinking it will change my financial situation. Ha!*

Toward the end of our visit, I considered the trip costs my brothers had incurred. One had airfare expenses. My other brother and his family had rented a minivan. *Father, it cost more for my children and me to fly here than the rest of the family combined. Our airfare, car rental, overnight motel, and all other expenses were just over $1400. And You provided all of it in advance!*

Now I sheepishly sat down to talk with God about the thirty dollars. *Father, I disobeyed You by not giving that "blessing money" to Pam and Randy when we visited them. Please forgive me for making excuses. Forgive me for not sending it later on. I was afraid of not having enough money for our trip to my parents. I doubted Your ability to provide for us. Please forgive me. I'm ashamed and embarrassed by my behavior. I want to make this right with You and with Pam and Randy.* God lifted my burden as I received His full forgiveness.

As I wrote out the thirty-dollar check, God said, "Write a letter explaining all this to Pam."

*Why? She doesn't know anything about it. She doesn't need to know. I can just send the check and thank her again for the great time we had at her home.*

"Tell her. You need to do it."

*How can I explain this mess? What will Pam think of me?*

I resisted for days and felt miserable. Finally I wrote and told her the whole story. "Please forgive me, Pam," I ended the letter, "for disobeying God and depriving you of God's blessing." As I wrote that letter, God revealed the mighty deliverance He had worked in my life. My intense fear of running out of money, which had plagued me for years, was completely gone. My fear of spending any money God provided was gone. My fear that God's supply for me would run out was gone.

*Father, throughout this whole year, You've faithfully supplied our every need: car repair, couch, grocery gift certificates, people who cared for us during my surgery, our trip to Pam's, and travel to my parents' anniversary celebration. Thank You for not instantly supplying everything we needed. Thank You for every circumstance during these months that has brought me to this deeper place of trusting You. Father, now I know without a doubt that You will provide for all my needs, in Your time and in Your way. You have set me free to enjoy Your present provision and share it with others. You have delivered me from the fear of future lack.*

### Answered Prayers

God miraculously answered many prayers for our family. However, one long-standing prayer remained unanswered.

In 1995, God had healed Rachel of a horrible four-month-long headache. But six months later, in August 1995, Rachel got another dreadful headache. *Oh no. How long will this one last? The doctors never figured out what caused her other headache. Father, You are the only One who can heal her.*

One morning as I prayed for Rachel, God said, "Linda, you give up too quickly in your battle against the Enemy. You must learn to stand firm. Hang on to My promises and persevere in prayer. I will teach you how to wrestle in prayer." Slowly, I began to recognize Satan's lies and stand against them. God's Word became my offensive weapon in fighting the Enemy. As God taught me to persevere in other areas of my life, He helped me stand in faith for Rachel's healing as well.

When our car broke down on the highway and needed a new engine, God taught me to trust Him. *Father, we depend on You to heal Rachel. You are the Great Physician.*

Rachel's head hurt all the time. During the autumn months. Over Thanksgiving. Throughout the Christmas holidays. All winter long. Her head ached continually. Persevering prayer was hard work, because we saw no change in her condition.

Through the delay in buying our couch, God taught me His timing is perfect. *Father, Your ways are always best. I trust Your timing for healing Rachel.* When God revealed that thanking Him in advance for airline tickets would honor Him, my prayers for Rachel changed. *Father, You are teaching us to walk by faith. Thank You for Rachel's healing before I see it.* As I battled fear on our trip to Pam's, I realized the spiritual war raging against Rachel. *Father, You defeated Satan when Jesus died on the cross. You won the victory so that Rachel can receive healing. Our hope is completely in You.*

Rachel's headache persisted during my parents' anniversary celebration and our vacation with them. "I'm not sure my headache will ever go away," Rachel confided in me, "but God healed me before and He can do it again."

*Father, thank You for embracing Rachel with Your love during this difficult time. Please be her daily source of strength. No one loves her as much as You do.*

Twenty-four hours a day, seven days a week, Rachel's headache plagued her continuously for eleven months. *Father, how long until You answer our prayers? We know You can heal Rachel and we believe You will. But when, Lord? You've deepened our trust in You. Even though we don't see any outward change, we know You are at work. Help us stand firm and not waver. Our hope is in You alone.*

One July afternoon, while riding in our car, Rachel exclaimed, "Mom, my headache is only a 'seven' on the headache scale." Before we got home, it was a "three."

Later, Rachel shouted, "My headache is gone! It's totally gone!" Her eyes sparkled and her countenance beamed as she romped around the house. Timothy, Jonathan and I hugged her and together praised God.

"Thank You for healing me, God!" Rachel rejoiced. "It's so good to be rid of that awful headache."

"Father, thank You for healing Rachel," I said, as tears of joy ran down my cheeks. "Thank You for answering our prayers. You are so good. You never change. You were the same, before healing Rachel, as You are right now. We give You all the glory."

"God built my trust in Him through these troubling times with my horrible headache," Rachel told her friends. "He has perfect timing in every situation. Whether you know it or not, God is caring for you all the time."

*Father, thank You for pouring out Your compassion on Rachel during these eleven painful months. Thank You for strengthening her faith. And thank You for teaching me to pray persistently and stand firm against the Enemy.* As I continued thanking God, He reminded me of a prayer I had prayed at the beginning of 1996: "Father, please revolutionize my prayer life this year." *Father, You've sure answered that prayer! You've used each hard situation this year to draw me closer to You. Please continue to change me. I welcome Your refining work in my life. Help me live in greater dependence upon You.*

* * *

1. What are some reasons for giving thanks to God? What reasons does Psalm 136:1 give? How would developing a daily habit of giving thanks to God influence your outlook on life? What's the purpose of thanking God in advance, before you know the outcome?

2. Give an example in your life when you had to persevere in prayer. What did God teach you during the delay that you might not have learned if He had answered immediately?

3. What fears do you face about money? How does the fear of future lack creep into your life? How do you prevent these fears from overtaking you?

*Father, help me run to You for refuge and find safety in Your loving arms.*

# Chapter Seven

# God Is Faithful

*The LORD's lovingkindnesses indeed never
cease, for His compassions never fail.
They are new every morning; Great is Your
faithfulness* (Lamentations 3:22-23 NASB).

## Trust Me

While my children took a trip with their dad in August
1996, I spent five days on a personal retreat at a place
called Pacem in Terris (Peace on Earth). *Father, the birthday
money You provided in June through Gail now gives me these
precious days alone with You.* I stayed in a hermitage: a rustic
cabin with a bed, a rocking chair, and a screened-in porch.
I had plenty of time to listen to God and pour out my heart
to Him. I felt wrapped up in His love.

One afternoon in the silence, my Father spoke tenderly
to me. "I have loved you with an everlasting love, Linda.
You cannot begin to grasp how much I love you and how
I've watched over you. You are beautiful to Me, My child.
You honor and praise Me with your life. I will not abandon

you. I will not leave you without hope. Only trust Me. Put your full confidence in Me and see what I will do.

"Trust Me. Don't try to figure everything out. Only trust Me. I will not lead you on a wrong or hurtful path. Trust Me. Keep your eyes on Me. Be attentive to My voice. I know the plans I have for you, to give you a future and a hope.

"In every situation, you can totally depend on Me. Look with the eyes of faith, not with your own understanding. Remember My faithfulness to you in the past. Know that I, the Lord, do not change."

I returned home, refreshed by the Lord and determined to trust Him more than ever in our daily situations. Living within welfare regulations was a walk of faith. Caseworkers gave conflicting explanations on how the rules worked, but one message came through loud and clear: "Do what we say or lose your benefits." For years I'd felt like I was walking across thin ice, terrified of accidentally falling through.

During 1996, the White House and Congress championed "ending welfare as we know it." They strove to dismantle the system but did not grasp the repercussions for those receiving assistance. I felt like a pawn in a heated political chess game. As legislators proposed radical welfare reform, it was a walk of faith for me to trust God with my family's future.

*Father, I feel so helpless. How will the proposed changes affect our family? Will there be sudden drastic cuts? How will we manage? I'm glad You are in control. You've been faithful in the past to meet all our needs. Welfare has been part of Your provision. You've also provided work for me during these years on welfare that has not compromised my primary commitment to my children. You've even made it possible for me to homeschool.*

*Your plans for us have been far beyond anything I imagined. You know the future, Father. I'm trusting You to lead us off the welfare system in Your time and in Your way.*

On Christmas Day 1996, I praised God for the precious gift of His Son, Jesus. I meditated on God's goodness. *Father, You are completely good. In every circumstance of my life, You have always been good to me.* As I worshiped, God spoke to my heart.

"1997 will be your year of deliverance from the welfare system. It will take a miracle, and I will do it. Just as I rescued the Israelites from their bondage in Egypt, so I will rescue you from the welfare system. My plans for you are good. Trust Me to act on your behalf. I am the Miracle Worker."

*Father, I welcome Your deliverance! I trust You completely. You are and always will be my provider—not welfare or work. Thank You for the good things You have planned for us in 1997. It will be a year of rescue and deliverance, of new hopes and dreams.*

### Stirring the Nest

"Will you go out without knowing?" my devotional book challenged me on January 3, 1997. It recounted how Abraham followed God's command to leave his homeland and go to a place he didn't know. *Father, I don't know where I'm going. I don't know how You'll get us off welfare. Please give me the grace to follow as You lead. Please create radical faith in me. I want to be fully abandoned to You.*

I constantly thought about God's promise to deliver us from the welfare system this year but didn't tell anyone about it. *The welfare system is so entangling. It seems impossible to get out of its grip. Father, how and when will You rescue us?* God spoke again through Abraham's life. "Is anything too hard for the LORD?" (Genesis 18:14). It was impossible for Abraham and his wife Sarah to have a baby in their old age, but God made it possible. *Is getting us off welfare too hard for the Lord? No! You already know Your plan to make it happen. Please help me trust You.*

For several months, God has impressed a specific Bible scene on my mind. During a raging storm, Peter climbed out of the boat and walked on the water toward Jesus, after Jesus said, "Come" (Matthew 14:22-31). *Father, that picture relates to us getting off welfare. It seems dangerous to step outside the boat, off welfare. Help me hear Your voice, fix my eyes firmly on You, and step out when You call me.*

I started a home business, thinking it would be God's way to rescue us from the welfare system. It totally flopped. *Our deliverance will have to be Your plan at Your time, Father. I can't make it happen. I commit all my future decisions to You. Help me trust You completely.*

Before each school year began, I specifically asked God for guidance in homeschooling decisions. This year I homeschooled Jonathan and Rachel while Timothy attended ninth grade at the public high school. I often brought Rachel and Jonathan with me to church, where I continued a second year of internship. They studied in a nearby room. I could check their progress, yet still carry out my internship responsibilities.

One January day, Timothy asked, "Mom, can I be homeschooled again?" His unexpected question unnerved me.

"You have to finish ninth grade at the high school," I replied, "and I don't know after that." When he asked several more times that month, I knew I needed to pray about it again.

*Father, the thought of homeschooling Timothy in high school overwhelms me. It's more than I can handle. How can I make any decisions for the future when I don't know what I'll be doing once we're off welfare? I'm listening for Your voice.* I prayed for weeks. God was silent.

In February, some of my internship responsibilities were eliminated. *Father, why is this happening? It feels like a rug has been pulled out from under my feet.*

"Cling to Me," God responded. "Your identity is in Me, not in what you do. I love you and have good plans for you."

*Father, I give You total access to my life. Please mold me according to Your purposes.*

As I spent time in God's presence seeking His direction, He stirred my passion for teaching. *Father, I have a burning desire to anchor people in Your Word and help them apply it to their daily lives. That's why I love working in ACTS as part of my internship. I want to invest in these students' lives. Are You leading me to expand my involvement in ACTS?*

My desire to teach continued to grow. In March, I arranged a meeting with the pastors to discuss possible job opportunities in ACTS after my internship ended. We brainstormed many potential ideas. As I prayed that night, God gave me an overall vision for ACTS Student Ministries, the hands-on application of classroom instruction. As He flooded my mind with ideas, I outlined a two-year program. I presented this plan to the ACTS staff. They heartily approved.

*Father, Your plans for Student Ministries seem so clear. What are Your plans for me? Will I work in ACTS after internship?*

"As I look ahead at my future, all I see is dense fog," I told a friend. "Every area of my life is unsettled. I don't know what's ahead in homeschooling or in my final months of internship. I feel like the ground under me is shifting and I'm about to fall flat on my face." *And Father, I still don't know Your plan for getting us off welfare. What will life be like once we're off welfare? How will I support my children?*

As we prayed together, God brought a Bible passage to her mind. "Listen to these verses," she encouraged me. "God wants you to see what He is doing in your life right now." She read Deuteronomy 32:10-12 (NASB):

> *"He found him in a desert land, And in the howling waste of a wilderness; He encircled him, He cared for him, He guarded him as the pupil of His eye. Like an eagle that stirs up its nest, That hovers over its young, He spread His wings and caught them, He carried them on His pinions. The Lord alone guided him, And there was no foreign god with him."*

*Father, You have watched over us during the past nine years. You have protected us and tenderly cared for us. Now You are stirring my nest; You are unsettling me. You are bringing radical change. You will carry me and keep me from falling. You are moving me out of the security of the welfare system into a deeper security in You.*

### Open Eyes

I longed to see my dear friend Pam and talk heart-to-heart. Eight months had passed since we'd visited her family. We kept in touch by phone, but it wasn't the same as being together. One day a mutual friend asked about Pam. After updating him, I sighed, "I sure wish I could see Pam. It would be a bright spot in this long cold winter."

"Have you considered flying out to see her?" he asked.

"No. I can't afford those outrageous fares." His question lingered in my mind all day long. If I could get a ticket for $100 I'd definitely go.

I called Pam that night. "What would you think about me flying out to visit you?"

"Really? You'd do that?" she asked eagerly.

"If I can get a low fare."

"Sometimes they go down to ninety-nine dollars during price wars," she encouraged.

"I'm sure there's a good deal out there. I'll keep you posted," I promised.

The lowest fare I found was $327. *That price is exorbitant! It's more than I've ever paid to fly anywhere in the country.*

"You already have the money to go," God whispered to me. "I provided it for you at Christmas." He reminded me of money I'd saved in one of my white envelopes as a buffer against sudden cuts in the welfare system.

*But Father, we might need that money for food or clothes. Wouldn't I be wasting it by buying an airline ticket?*

God directed me to 2 Kings 6:15-17. Elisha's servant panicked because their enemies surrounded them. Elisha prayed, "O LORD, open his eyes that he may see," and God let the servant see the unseen horses and chariots He had provided to protect them. The story is about seeing the unseen, about seeing in the spiritual realm. *Father, please open my eyes to Your abundant resources for us. I give You all my fears about sudden welfare reductions. Forgive me for clinging to Your provision instead of clinging to You.*

A few days later, I made reservations to fly to Pam's in April. Friends offered to care for my children so I could spend four days with her. *Father, You are my provider. Sometimes You provide through bargains and sometimes You supply extravagantly. Your provision for this trip expresses*

*Your loving care for me. Taking this trip will show that I trust You for our future needs.*

### Needed Oasis

Before visiting Pam, I had to endure another annual AFDC re-certification interview. My stomach churned as I drove to the welfare office. Living on welfare was like playing a game without knowing all the rules. I could be eliminated from the program by accidentally breaking a rule I'd never been told about. *Father, how long until You rescue us from this demeaning system?*

The caseworker studied my paperwork. "Your assets are over the limit," he concluded.

"How can that be? My income hasn't changed at all."

"Your children's bank accounts put you over the $1000 family asset limit."

"You told me their paper route income wouldn't lower our AFDC grant."

"Their *income* doesn't count. But their *savings accounts* are included in your total family assets." After three years of saving part of their paper route money, my three children each had over $100 in the bank. Their savings plus mine put our family assets over $1000. That would automatically terminate our AFDC grant.

"You mean we're penalized because I'm teaching my children to save part of their income rather than spend it all?"

"Yeah, I guess you could say that's how the system works."

"That's crazy! What am I supposed to do now?" *Father, what will happen to us if they cut off our AFDC? Please open my eyes to see Your unlimited resources.*

"There's a three-week period before any action is taken. Pay two months' rent or make extra utility payments. Buy things in bulk. Buy new bikes for your kids—anything to get your bank balance reduced. Keep all your receipts."

During the next two weeks, I stocked up on toothpaste, soap, deodorant, toilet paper, underwear, and socks. I paid two months' rent. I wrote checks for every purchase and kept each receipt. My anxiety increased as our money decreased. Before I mailed in my receipts, I received a notice from the county: "Your AFDC assistance is terminated immediately. You failed to turn in the required forms."

I frantically called my caseworker. "What does this notice mean?"

"I didn't get your bank verification form," he said coldly.

"What form is that? I've never heard of it. You told me to send you all my receipts by this Friday."

"I don't need your receipts," he said, his voice filled with condescension. "Go to your bank. Have them complete the verification form stating the current amount in your checking account. Send *that* to me immediately."

Perplexed, I hung up the phone. *This doesn't make sense. Why did he tell me earlier to keep all my receipts if he doesn't need them?* Suddenly, his indirect message became clear: buy costly items, save the receipts, turn in the verification form with the lower bank balance to re-qualify for assistance, then return the merchandise for a full refund. I felt nauseous. *No wonder there's an outcry for welfare reform. Oh God, deliver us quickly.*

The next week I flew to Pam's. Her guest room felt like a shelter, a place of comfort in the midst of a raging storm. In contrast to the oppression I felt from the welfare system, my days with Pam provided life-giving conversation. We talked about our families, our hopes, and our dreams. We shared what God was teaching us through our struggles. I expressed misgivings about my future; Pam told of uncertainties in her life. We laughed, cried, and prayed together.

"I came here to encourage you, Pam," I said, "yet you've encouraged me. You are a dear friend. I want you to know how much I care about you."

"Linda, your willingness to spend your money to fly out here speaks volumes about caring for me," she replied.

"Pam, your home has been a sanctuary for me, full of God's presence and peace. My confidence in God has been refreshed during our days together. You are a precious blessing in my life." *Thank You, Father, that our friendship is anchored in You. We're free to share our hopes and fears because we know we're loved and accepted by You and by each other. Thank You for providing this oasis, this quiet, tender time together.*

### Are You Willing?

"Linda," God asked, "are you willing to follow Me fully, even if it means having no financial security in this world and walking by faith financially?"

*Father, I assumed that when You led me off the welfare system, it would be to a place of financial stability and security. Now it seems You're calling me to a deeper walk of faith. I'm afraid. Please reveal this resistance deep within my heart.*

"Follow Me, Linda," my heavenly Father beckoned. "Follow Me fully and I will provide for you as I have in the past. Don't look to a job to be your provider. Don't look to people. Look to Me and continue to follow as I lead you."

I recounted God's abundant provision during the past

nine years. I remembered 2 Chronicles 16:9 (NASB): "For the eyes of the LORD move to and fro throughout the earth that He may strongly support those whose heart is completely His." *Father, I've seen Your faithfulness. Why do I hesitate to trust You now?* I struggled with that question for an entire week. *Father, I don't understand this battle raging in my heart. Please help me.*

God had more questions for me to answer.

"Have I ever let you down in providing for your needs?"

*No.*

"Could you have found a home like this by yourself?"

*No, I was desperate for You to act. It's far beyond my expectations.*

"Have your children had clothes, jackets, boots, mittens, whatever they've needed for each season of the year?"

*Yes, You've provided wonderfully.*

"Could you have saved up the money for the Mexico mission trip?"

*Absolutely not. We only had four months to raise nearly $800.*

"Could you have flown to visit Pam apart from My provision?"

*No. That ticket was paid for by gifts You supplied.*

"Could you have saved the money to visit your parents for their fiftieth anniversary, been able to bless them with that special overnight trip, and had it all paid for before going?"

*Never, Lord. It was impossible for me, but You came through.*

"Have you lacked any necessary materials for home-schooling?"

*No, my children have not lacked anything.*

"Would you have the white '87 Dodge Aries without My intervention?"

*No. You provided a buyer for the Citation, Wes's willingness to lease me the white car, and Promised Land Motors.*

"Would you have a computer without My provision?"

*No. And You provided two other improved models since the first, and a computer desk, too.*

"Would you have had the money to pay your tuition for ACTS apart from Me prompting churches to invite you to speak?"

*No. You supplied all my tuition in that way.*

"Have you or your children ever had a physical need that I have not provided for in some way?"

*No, Lord, You have been totally faithful.*

"My child, why are you holding back? Have I been your faithful God or not? Have I provided abundantly or not? Have I demonstrated my loving-kindness to you or not? I, the Lord, do not change. As I was in the past, I will be in the future. I long to fully support you with My unlimited resources, but I cannot while you are holding back. Haven't I proven My faithfulness throughout these years? Even the money you receive from AFDC comes from My hand. Health insurance, food stamps, Rent Assistance, Energy Assistance: it all filters through My hands to you. What is holding you back from total abandonment to Me?"

All at once I saw my unbelief. I checked the dictionary to fully understand the meaning of the word.

**unbelief:** *the condition of being unpersuadeable; denotes obstinacy*

**obstinate:** *perversely adhering to an opinion or course in spite of reason, arguments, or persuasion*

The truth pierced my heart. I stood convicted of my sin.

*Oh, Father, forgive me. Even with Your abundant provision, I doubt Your love for me. I doubt Your willingness to keep on providing. Forgive me for questioning Your character. You're showing me that unbelief is a choice I make. I confess my sin of unbelief: choosing not to believe what You say in Your Word, choosing to disregard all the evidence of Your faithfulness in my life.* I cried out in anguish over my sin. *Forgive me, Father, for grieving You. Cleanse me from my sin and forgive me because of Jesus' sacrifice for me on the cross.* I received God's complete forgiveness and sat quietly before Him for a long time.

As I waited in His presence, a new confidence rose up within me. *Father, I refuse to hold back any longer. I will take this leap of faith into Your arms. I am willing to follow You fully, even if it means no financial security in this world and having to walk by faith financially. I declare that You are my Provider. I trust You to supply my family's needs. Your faithfulness will continue because You do not change. Thank You for bringing me to this deeper place of dependence on You.*

### Mounting Tension

For months I'd prayed about homeschooling decisions but had no clear answers. *Father, what is Your unique plan for Timothy? Help me understand his needs. Help me see him as you do. Please show me Your plans for homeschooling any of my children in the fall.*

In May, the pastors at church conferred with me about a potential position developing and leading the ACTS Student Ministries program. "I'd also like to teach more courses in ACTS and expand prayer support for the school," I said. "I could work fifteen hours a week."

"What do you need financially?" one pastor asked.

"God has miraculously provided for us during the past nine years," I replied. "I don't know what our actual needs will be. Probably $1000 a month."

"I'll have to discuss this with other leaders and get back to you," he said. *Father, I'm trusting You.*

At a church staff meeting, a visiting pastor spoke encouraging words to me. "God will use you to bring hope to others," he said. "The consistency of your life and your faith will be a testimony. God has called you to more than what is in your heart right now. He is going to expand your vision. It will come out of relationship with Him, by praying about what you do, and taking time to seek His face."

*Father, thank You for giving me hope in this confusing time. Thank You for Your good plans for my life.*

As I kept seeking God for His homeschooling plan for our family, God changed *me.* By late June, I was *willing* to teach all three children at home. That thought had paralyzed me in the past. But I still had no specific direction for Timothy.

"Mom, do you know yet who's going to be homeschooled?" Jonathan asked one summer day.

"I'm still praying about it," I replied, "but it might be all three of you."

"But I want to be 'public schooled,'" he insisted. "I have to go there."

*What's going on, Lord? I've never seen Jonathan so adamant.*

Later that night I spent time praying about Jonathan. *What is Your plan for him, Father?*

"I'm sending Jonathan as a missionary to the public school," God said clearly. "Let him go."

For the first time in weeks, deep peace flooded my heart. *Father, thanks for revealing Your plans for Jonathan.*

The next morning I talked with Jonathan. "You'll carry God's love to your classmates at school like a hose carries water to the garden," I explained.

"Actually, Mom, it would hurt to get sprayed by a hose," he replied. "I'll be more like a sprinkler."

*Father, You've obviously been speaking to Jonathan!* When I called the school to register him, fifth grade was full. I put his name on the waiting list. *Father, if You want Jonathan there, please make a place for him.*

Trying to figure out my financial future exhausted me. I made countless phone calls and discovered the financial backlash of moving from welfare to work. Earning $1000 a month would terminate our $621 AFDC grant, our $250 a month in food stamps, and our health insurance. My rent portion would increase ten times its current amount. Once off AFDC, I would receive child-support, but that would increase my monthly rent portion more. *If I work at ACTS, we'll end up living on less than we do right now. I feel trapped. How will I ever get off the welfare system?*

I read and reread Philippians 4:6-7:

> Do not be anxious about anything, but in everything, by prayer and petition, with thanksgiving, present your requests to God. And the peace of God, which transcends all understanding, will guard your hearts and your minds in Christ Jesus.

*Father, I want to be a living example of these verses. Teach me how to trust You in the midst of uncertainty. I need Your peace.*

Staff changes at church in July postponed my meeting with the pastors about the ACTS position. Agitated about my indefinite future, I wrote them a brief note. "I could work up to twenty hours a week," I explained, "to earn more income."

*Father, last December You promised to rescue us from the welfare system. Now it's August. Why are You silent? Why can't I hear Your voice? How can I make any plans for the future when I don't have a clue about Your plans for us?*

An unexpected letter arrived from a family unaware of my distress. "Please use this money to get away alone, Linda," they wrote. "We'll take care of your children."

*Thank You for this gift, Father. I know just where I'll go—back to Pacem in Terris—to be alone with You. I know I'll hear Your voice there.*

* * *

1. Share some examples of God's faithfulness in your life. Even with those experiences, what makes it difficult for you to trust Him now?

2. When have you wondered if God would get tired of caring for you? Have you feared He might stop providing for you? What evidence do these verses give of God's long-term care: Exodus 16:4,35; Deuteronomy 8:2-4; Isaiah 46:3-4? How can these examples encourage you?

3. What are the benefits of turning to God in our crises? How have you experienced this in your life?

*Father, please reveal Your long-term faithfulness to me.*

## Chapter Eight

# God Keeps His Promises

*The LORD is faithful to all his promises and*
*loving toward all he has made*
*(Psalm 145:13).*

### My Need to Know

*Father, thank You for Pacem in Terris, a place of solitude*
*with You. I give You all my worries and fears. I surrender myself*
*to You. Please work deeply in my heart during these three days*
*alone with You.*

I read the biblical account of the Exodus, the picture
God had given me of rescuing us from welfare. At the
edge of the Red Sea, Moses told the Israelites, "Do not be
afraid. Stand firm and you will see the deliverance the
LORD will bring you today" (Exodus 14:13). *They could not*
*bring about their own deliverance. They could only cry out to*
*God. Oh Father, please rescue us!*

As I walked through the fields and by the lake, God
comforted me. "Don't be anxious, Linda. I am your

Father and I care for you. I know your needs. Don't worry about anything."

*Father, please forgive me for worrying. I've been focusing on my situation instead of on You. I give You everything I'm anxious about: getting off welfare, homeschooling decisions, and the possible job at ACTS.*

I wanted answers about our immediate future. My heavenly Father met my deeper need to be enveloped in His love during this distressing time. Whether sleeping or awake, I deeply sensed God's presence and comforting love.

"I came here for specific answers to urgent decisions in my life," I told the director of Pacem in Terris. "God has been silent. I still don't know what to do."

"When a carpenter builds a house, he doesn't carry around all his tools for the entire job," she explained. "He only carries what he needs for the part he's working on. Trust God, Linda. Thank Him that He will tell you what you need to know when you need to know it."

*Father, I know You have the answers I need. More than answers, I need You.*

I left Pacem in Terris without clear direction for Timothy. *Father, school starts in two weeks. Do I teach him at home or keep him in public school? I need to hear from You.*

On August 19, 1997, I drove to church for a meeting about the job at ACTS. *Finally, we'll discuss this position and find a workable arrangement. Father, I'm trusting You.* An emergency at church that morning canceled our meeting. I couldn't concentrate on a single thing for the rest of the day. *Father, I feel like I'm falling into a bottomless pit. I have no answers about my future. Time is running out. I feel totally helpless. I can't live this way any longer.*

Suddenly I heard myself whining and complaining,

just like the Israelites at the edge of the Red Sea. I started crying. *Father, forgive me. I've been trying to find my own way across this Red Sea. Forgive me for taking my eyes off of You. Forgive me for forgetting what You can do.*

I resolved to make an immediate change. *Father, I choose to trust You. This testing time is part of Your design to strengthen me. Thank You for what You're doing in me in this situation. I will rejoice on this side of the Red Sea,* before I see *Your mighty deliverance.*

A few days later, a visiting pastor spoke at our church. "When the apostle Paul told his friend Timothy to 'come before winter,' he was describing a specific time period when Timothy could safely travel there," he explained. "In relationships and missions, there are seasons of opportunity that can be life-changing. They are 'come before winter' times. They don't last indefinitely; they need to be embraced."

God whispered to me, "This is a 'come before winter' time for Timothy. Do whatever it takes to teach him at home all year and watch what I will do in his life."

*Father, thank You for Your clear answer. You do tell me what I need to know when I need to know it. I embrace this year with Timothy at home.*

### Inner Turmoil

Tears filled my eyes as I drove to meet my friend Gail for lunch. *My whole world is caving in. I still don't know how God will get us off the welfare system. I don't know if I'll be working at ACTS this fall. I don't even know if Wes will ever get the rust holes repaired on this car.* Thinking about the car reminded me of those irksome "car conversations" with Timothy during the past two months. *His opinion of our car sank once he drove that brand new, accessory-filled car for driver education training. Just remembering his words aggravates me.*

"I wish our car had a tape deck," fifteen-year-old Timothy said one day as I drove along the highway.

"You and I have different priorities in a car," I asserted. "When I got this car, I wanted it to be safe, affordable, and dependable. I thought the AM-FM radio was great. Our last car only had an AM radio. Someday, when *you* buy a car, a tape deck will probably be a high priority. It's not even *on* my list."

"This car has such a bumpy ride," Timothy remarked another day while I drove. "Mom, when do you think we might get a different car?"

"*This* car is a wonderful gift from God to our family," I retorted. "It's only ten years old. We can get at least 50,000 more miles out of it." It already had 150,000 miles. "For five years it has served us well, and Wes has faithfully repaired it. I'm content with our car and don't have *any* plans for a new one." *Besides, this car is paid for. And it's the nicest car we've ever owned.*

Each time Timothy pointed out some minor deficiency in our car, my irritation increased. *His concerns are so trivial compared to the enormous decisions I'm facing.*

As I drove him on an errand another day, he wistfully sighed again, "I wish we had a tape deck in this car."

"Timothy!" I snapped, "*You* can be praying about our next car." *I* certainly wasn't. I only wanted him to be quiet. From then on, anytime he commented about our car, I lashed out, "*You* can be praying about our next car." It effectively ended all conversation.

*Being with Gail today will be a wonderful diversion from all the stress I'm facing. We haven't seen each other in months.*

Our quiet corner of the restaurant provided a perfect place to talk. Near the end of our meal, all my inner fears erupted like lava from a volcano. "I'm so afraid of the future, Gail," I confided. "My life feels totally out of control."

As we drove back to Gail's house, worries kept gushing from my mouth. "Yesterday Wes did emergency repairs on my car. It'll be weeks until he can work on it again. For months, other commitments have prevented him from repairing rusted areas. I'm afraid he won't get it done before winter. It's just one more problem I can't do anything about," I sobbed. "I've never felt so helpless in my entire life."

As we entered Gail's driveway, she said, "Wait here in the car. I want to take you somewhere." A few minutes later she got back into the car. "Here," she said as she dropped a set of keys into my hands. "These are the keys to your next car." My mouth dropped open.

"As we left the restaurant after lunch," Gail explained, "God told me, 'Linda needs your car.' I didn't know what that meant, but when you started talking about your car, I knew God was at work. I recently bought the car we're riding in, but haven't sold my old one yet. I'll drive you out to see it."

Gail's "old" car was a luxury '94 Chrysler Concorde. The dashboard looked like a flight instrument panel. I cautiously drove it back to her house.

"I'll gather the papers and sign the car over to you right now!" Gail exclaimed, as we walked into her home.

"Gail," I stammered, "Wait! I'm overwhelmed. My head is spinning." I paused, trying to collect my thoughts. "Gail, let's slow down a little. In practical terms, my children and I are going camping this week. My car has a trailer hitch; the Concorde doesn't. Let's keep your car here and work out the details after my trip."

I drove my car home, amazed by God's goodness. Yet one thought troubled me. *Is the Concorde suitable for our family? It has less room inside than our car. Father, You know what's best for us. I leave it all in Your hands.*

"Can we drive out to see the car now?" my children pleaded when I told them about it that evening. We laughed and praised God for His wonderful surprise.

Suddenly, I remembered my "car conversations" with Timothy. Turning toward him, I gently asked, "Timothy, have you been praying about our next car?"

With a twinkle in his eye and a slight grin at the corner of his mouth, he paused and answered, "Well...some."

### Daily Reminder

"I'm wondering if the Concorde is the best car for your growing family," Gail said on the phone the next morning. "What would you think of me selling it and helping you buy a more family-friendly car?"

"That sounds great," I replied. "A bigger car would give more space for us and other kids, too." *Thanks for giving Gail this idea, Lord.*

"Start looking at cars to see what you like," Gail said.

"Okay," I sighed, "but it'll be a long, slow process. I know nothing about cars." *Tomorrow we go camping. Then I'll need to prepare for homeschool. This car search is just one more thing to do, one more unknown in my life. Father, help me not to worry, but trust You instead. Thanks for Your good plans for our family.*

After our camping trip, I talked with one family who

owned a van. *I'm so frustrated. I hardly have time to get informed, much less look at cars.*

Gail called again. "My son Tyson has decided to take on this project for you," she said. "He needs to know what you want in a car."

"I'd like a minivan that's safe, dependable, and has no rust," I replied without hesitation. "Timothy wants a car with a tape deck," I added, sharing bits of our "car conversations."

"Tyson will see what cars he can come up with," Gail said. "Tell Timothy if the car you decide on doesn't have a tape deck, we'll have one put in for him."

*Father, thank You for Tyson and his practical knowledge about cars. Guide him to one that's good for our family. Please bless him for his willingness to help us.*

Five days later, Gail called. "Tyson checked all over the metro area and found twenty possible vans," she reported. "He drove ten vans and has narrowed it down to one. It's here in our town. When can you come and look at it?"

"We can all come on Saturday morning," I said, wanting to go as a family.

"It's an '88 Dodge conversion van with 100,000 miles," Gail said. "The owner used it for hunting and fishing. Tyson will explain more when you're here."

*What's a conversion van? Two half-vehicles joined together? A van used for hunting and fishing? I just know there's deer blood in the carpet. Father, help me trust You.*

"The van is dependable and easy to drive," Tyson told us on Saturday. "If you decide you're not interested, I might buy it myself."

I scanned the car lot, trying to locate a conversion van. I was not prepared for what the dealer drove up in front of us: a dark blue Dodge minivan with light blue pinstriping, running boards, fog lights, and no rust. *An '88 in Minnesota with no rust? It looks brand new.* Dark blue carpet. Blue-gray seats. Navy blue curtains hanging from wooden panels above the side windows. A removable table. *This is like being on a treasure hunt.* One bench seat in the middle and a cushioned board behind it in place of another seat. The middle seat could lay flat and, with the board, make a six-foot bed. Reading lights by each seat; cup holders, too. Captain's chairs up front, able to recline as well as face backwards. *I've never seen anything like this!* A sun roof. And a tape deck with a built-in wooden cassette tape holder. *Timothy will love this.* Rear window wiper and defroster. A trailer hitch and electrical hookups already attached. *Perfect for pulling our camper.* And cruise control. *Great for long trips.* On the test drive, I immediately felt comfortable driving it.

"Let's go talk with the dealer," Gail urged, as my children continued exploring the van. In the office, Gail wrote a check and gave it to the dealer. Then she took the keys and handed them to me!

*What an incredible God You are! What a precious sister in the Lord Gail is! What a gift!*

We marveled at God's miracle as we ate lunch together to celebrate. *That beautiful blue van outside is really ours! And all this happened in two weeks.*

Gail looked at me and said, "Linda, I felt God saying that at this particular time you needed a tangible, daily reminder of His love and faithfulness. This van can be that reminder every time you drive it."

*Father, bless Gail for her generosity and her sensitivity to Your voice. Thanks for showing Timothy that You hear his prayers and care about him. How abundantly You provide when we leave the choice to You.*

"Thank You, Father, for blessing us with this new van," we prayed as a family. "Please give us many opportunities to share this story with others.

"Look at the van God's given us!" we shouted to our friends, Kelli and Bob, as we pulled into their driveway on our way home.

"What kind is it?" Bob asked.

"I don't know," I shrugged. Then I noticed a small ram on each side. "It's a Dodge Ram minivan," I announced.

Later that afternoon, Kelli asked, "Linda, when is a ram mentioned in the Bible?"

"When Abraham went to sacrifice his son, Isaac," I replied.

"Isaac asked where the lamb was for the sacrifice, and Abraham told him God would provide it," Kelli emphasized. "When the angel stopped Abraham from killing Isaac, Abraham saw a ram in the thicket and sacrificed it. He named that place 'The Lord Will Provide' [Genesis 22:14]. This is where God is first revealed as Jehovah-Jireh, the Lord our Provider."

And this is our testimony: God is our Jehovah-Jireh. In every situation, He knows our needs and provides abundantly. Would He have given us anything but a *Ram* van?

### Refiner's Fire

God had spoken clearly during the past two weeks. He opened a place for Jonathan at the public school. We prayed for him and commissioned him as a missionary. God specifically told me to homeschool Timothy during this "come before winter" season in his life. God miraculously provided the Ram van as a daily reminder of His love and faithfulness. Two days later He provided a buyer for our white car. *Father, You are caring for us. You are revealing Your plans in Your time.*

One question still plagued my thoughts. *God, how will You rescue us from the welfare system? Will it be through a job at ACTS? Or do You have some other plan?*

My fall calendar bulged with responsibilities. Teaching Timothy at home would require extra planning. Rachel would need my help with her studies. I would attend events at Jonathan's school. And I would need time to prepare for six speaking engagements. *So many needs clamor for my attention, Father. Please be Lord of my time.*

In early September, I met with two pastors about the ACTS position. *Father, I'm glad we can finally meet to discuss this.* First, one presented the salary package: a livable wage with health insurance for me. *Thank You, Father.* Then he handed me a job description. The position required twenty-five hours a week. ACTS Student Ministries was listed first, followed by multiple responsibilities in various areas of the church.

"I thought we were meeting today to discuss the ACTS position and outline a job description together," I said. "This job requires more hours than I want to work. We've never discussed most of the responsibilities listed here. Some of them conflict with my current commitments."

I quickly learned that the job description was non-negotiable. *What do I do now, God? It's all or nothing. I spent my final months of internship developing the fall Student Ministries program for ACTS. I don't want to abandon that now: ACTS begins in two weeks.* Since I felt God had given me a clear vision for ACTS Student Ministries last spring,

I agreed to what appeared to be an impossible job description. *Father, help me. The time demands of this job seem to conflict with the needs of my family.*

Juggling twenty-five hours of work plus home-schooling was difficult. I didn't have adequate time to prepare, teach, or review assignments with my children. They often struggled with their schoolwork alone.

My additional responsibilities at church pulled me in many different directions. Pressing needs in the church superseded my priorities in ACTS. Student Ministries got shortchanged of my focused attention. I worked extra hours, trying to get everything done. During my first six weeks on the job, I worked more than 200 hours, far beyond the stated job description of twenty-five hours a week.

Our family life suffered. I threw meals together at the last minute. The house was a mess. I had no time to run errands. We ran out of groceries and household supplies. All of us grew irritable. *Father, I need Your wisdom and strength to manage all of this. Have Your way with me. My time is in Your hands.*

Leading the annual overnight ACTS retreat required a large block of time. My six speaking engagements took extra time away from my family, too. *I'm gone more than I'm home with my children. I don't want to live this way.*

I burst into tears over little things. I couldn't think straight. My life was out of balance, headed for burnout. *Father, I feel like I'm going crazy. Help me lean on You. I want to be Spirit-led, not driven. Thank You for the daily reminder of Your faithfulness in the Ram van.*

I had the ability to carry out the full job description. The issue was this: raising my children and providing a secure, peaceful home environment were my top priorities. This job jeopardized those values. *Father, I prayed about each of these decisions. You revealed that I was to teach Timothy at home this year. You aligned my priorities with my children and homeschooling before I was offered this position. The demands of this job are pulling me away from the needs of my family. I feel like I'm sacrificing my children. Please help me through this. Thank You for using this painful situation to refine me.*

Besides these work struggles, I faced major conflicts with our upstairs neighbors. Blaring music in the middle of the night woke us up and prevented us from sleeping. Ear-splitting music during the day interfered with home-schooling. Local authorities advised me to call the police about the noise. That temporarily stopped the booming music, but increased our neighbors' animosity. The police recommended mediation; our neighbors refused. *Father, I feel like a prisoner in my own home. The tension here is unbearable.*

Then the owner put the house up for sale. *Now what's going to happen? Will we have to move? Father, please help me.* "In all these things, stand," God replied. "Stand firm." *Father, please bring good out of this. Thank You for how You're using this crisis to refine me.*

On November 4, I met with the pastors about my job. "I cannot continue the position outlined in this job description," I began. "These extra projects consume time and energy I need for the Student Ministries program. I can work totally in ACTS, or combine it with teaching in the church. I can work twenty hours a week maximum. Any additional hours are too big a price for my family to pay." After a lengthy discussion, the pastors agreed to think it over and meet again in the future.

Later that day I talked with Timothy. "I know these

past two months have been hard on all of us," I said. "If you could decide how and where I spend my time, how would you arrange it?"

"Mom, anyone can do the job you're doing at ACTS and church," he answered immediately, "but no one else can homeschool us."

*Father, thanks for Your encouragement through Timothy. It is a "come before winter" year for him. I will obey Your instruction to "do whatever it takes to teach him at home all year."*

A second meeting about my position was set for December 2. *Father, I give You all my anxieties about this job, money, and supporting my family. I want Your best for my children and me. My life is in Your hands. Thank You for this process I'm going through. Thank You for Your faithfulness.*

"You have two options," the pastor informed me. "Continue the job as originally stated, or work only in ACTS for thirteen hours a week at half the salary. Insurance will be provided either way. Take some time to think it over."

I left the five-minute meeting and burst into tears. *Father, help me. I know I can't handle the original job description. I've tried for three months with disastrous effects on my family. There's no middle ground here, no twenty-hour option. The thirteen-hour job would let me focus on ACTS, but the cut in salary terrifies me.*

The next morning, I dialed the phone. "Wes," I said, close to tears, "please tell me God loves me and has good plans for my life."

"He does love you, Linda, and His plans for you are very good," he reassured me. "What's going on?" He listened patiently as I explained my predicament. "Linda," he asked, "what is God saying to you through all this? Don't focus on people or your circumstances. The primary issue is this:

What does God want to do in you through this situation?"

Tears streamed down my face. I had no answer.

"Linda," Wes continued gently, "I believe you are at a crossroads. God wants to bring you to a place of trusting Him beyond yourself, beyond how much you think you can possibly trust Him." His words touched a place deep in my heart. I knew what he said was true. "Let me pray for you," he offered.

After I hung up the phone, I continued talking to God. *Father, I am at a crossroads of faith. Do I follow Your calling to ACTS and trust You to provide? That looks like financial suicide. Or do I continue this position that offers financial security yet hurts my family and derails me from following Your plans for us?*

God reminded me again of His promise: "For the eyes of the Lord move to and fro throughout the earth that He may strongly support those whose heart is completely His" (2 Chronicles 16:9 NASB). *Father, security comes from You, not from a paycheck. I want to fully follow You, no matter what. But if I take the thirteen-hour job at half salary, how can I manage financially?*

"The freedom you've enjoyed recently with a larger income is the same freedom you are to live in as you follow Me," my heavenly Father answered. "My unlimited resources in Christ are available to you."

*Father, You are the supplier of all my needs. You are working radical faith in me. Please give me the grace to walk by faith with my eyes fixed on You.*

"Have you reached your decision?" the pastor asked a few days later.

"Yes," I said confidently, "I'll work only in ACTS." As I spoke those words, a wave of peace swept over me.

"The change will become effective January 1," he replied.

*I'm following You, Lord. Thank You for leading me through these pressurized months. Thanks for Your refining work in my life.*

That afternoon I received a letter from the county: "Your food stamps case is immediately terminated. Your income is too high."

*This is going to be a walk of faith, isn't it, Father?*

## God's Miracle

During those turbulent fall months in 1997, fears about my unknown financial future assailed me. I felt like I was lost at sea on a puny raft, constantly battered by the waves. *Father, I'm clinging to You. You alone are my hope and security. Please bring me through this tumultuous storm.*

When my September AFDC check arrived, I put it all in the bank. *I can't spend this money. What if I have to return it to the county since I'm starting a job?* Then someone anonymously gave us $500. *Thank You, Father, for providing this money for our daily needs.*

As soon as I started my job, I called my caseworker. "I want to report some changes," I told her. "I now own an '88 Dodge Ram minivan. I sold our '87 Dodge Aries. And I have a job."

"What did you pay for the van?"

"Nothing. It was a gift."

"What? How much is it worth?"

"I don't know. It was a gift."

"How about the other car?"

"I sold it for $400, two days after we were given the van."

"These transactions must be verified. You must send proof that you own the van and don't own the Aries. Have you been paid yet from your job?"

"No, I'll be paid on the fifteenth and thirtieth of each month."

"How many hours will you work? How much will you be paid?" She questioned me incessantly, yet wouldn't explain how these changes would impact our family. "Your employer must complete a verification form," she insisted. "Send me a copy of your first paycheck as soon as you get it."

*Father, I'm afraid. How will all these changes affect us? Everything is so uncertain. Be my anchor in this unstable time.*

When I reported my first paycheck in mid-September, the caseworker stated, "Your AFDC case will close at the end of this month. The food stamp program follows different formulas, so you may still be eligible. Since you are working, we can continue some health insurance for you for a limited time."

*Father, You are caring for us. Please help me trust You.*

"When will child-support checks come directly to me?" I asked. During the years I received AFDC, the welfare system claimed all child-support payments. Now, with AFDC ending, I could receive future child-support payments.

"Once your AFDC case closes, I'll notify the Child-Support Collections Department," the worker replied. "They're changing to a state-wide system, so it could be six or eight weeks before you see a check."

*Father, that's a long time from now. Please provide for our needs. Thanks for this provision for our family.*

A few days later, I received a letter from the county. *It's* *probably the food stamp program, terminating our $254 monthly allowance.*

"Food stamp allotment levels have been readjusted by the government. Starting October 1, 1997, you will receive $408 in food stamps each month."

*Father, there's never been an increase like this since we started getting food stamps. Your timing is perfect, Your provision abundant.*

My six speaking engagements provided additional income. I spoke on the topics "Tired of Trying to Do it All" and "Single Parenting: God's Abundant Provision." *Father, You have a great sense of humor. I'm struggling with all this upheaval in my life, yet declaring Your faithfulness. Thank You for showing Your strength through my weakness.*

Each time I notified Rent Assistance of additional income, my fears increased. *What if my new rent skyrockets beyond what I can pay?*

In December, when I considered taking the smaller ACTS job, I worried about being able to make ends meet. Then someone sent us seventy-five dollars in grocery store gift certificates. *Father, thanks for this reminder of Your faithfulness. You never get tired of caring for us. Your resources never run out.*

The same day I accepted the thirteen-hour ACTS job at half salary, the food stamp termination notice arrived in the mail. *Father, I was counting on that $408 a month in food stamps. How will we ever have enough money for food?*

"I am your provider," God reminded me. "Look to Me for all your needs. You are done using food stamps even if you qualify for them in the future. I am rescuing you from the welfare system and setting you free."

Someone gave us a bag of potatoes and carrots.

Someone else gave us a bag of clothes. A friend sent me $175, her honorarium from speaking at a retreat. Someone sent us $100 in grocery store gift certificates. *Thank You, Father, for these reminders of Your faithfulness. You have resources I know nothing about.*

I thought about the stones of remembrance in the Bible in Joshua 4. After the Israelites miraculously crossed the Jordan River, God told them to set up huge stones from the river as continual reminders of what He had done for them. My friend Kelli brought us a bucket of gold-painted stones. "You need some visible reminders of God's faithfulness," she said. We displayed a stone for each provision we had received.

I notified Rent Assistance immediately of my impending salary cut. They reduced my January rent to reflect my decrease in income. I learned we could spend the food stamps still in my account. We continued to receive money gifts and grocery gift certificates. We placed stones of remembrance all over our house.

At the end of December, God opened my eyes to see the past four months from His perspective. The view was spectacular. Although I didn't know it at the time, the Ram van had been God's vehicle to catapult us off the welfare system. It was worth much more than the car-value limits imposed by AFDC. The Ram van, our daily reminder of God's faithfulness, closed my welfare case!

God had been actively involved in everything: arranging a livable salary at my job; allowing me to keep my September AFDC check of $621, since I reported the Ram van within ten days; additional income from speaking; child-support checks now sent to me; a huge increase in food stamps two months before they were terminated; keeping our rent at its lower rate in September and October, even though my income increased; a total of $225 in grocery gift certificates; and over $850 given to us throughout December.

This panoramic view proclaimed God's faithfulness. *Father, You kept Your promise! You delivered us from the welfare system this year. Your intricate timing and detailed plans amaze me. You have blessed us abundantly. You are holding us in the palm of Your hand.*

In 1988, when I first applied for AFDC, I had no choice but to trust God to care for us. During these nine-and-a-half years, God clearly revealed Himself as our Provider. Now I experienced His miraculous deliverance from the system that had been "part of His provision" for our family. *Thank You, Father, for rescuing us and setting us free. You have shown Yourself strong on our behalf. You are totally dependable. I willingly follow wherever You lead in our new venture of faith.*

\* \* \*

1. When in your life has trusting God felt like walking off the edge of a cliff? What step of faith did you take in your job or financially or with your family? What happened?

2. "The LORD is faithful to all his promises and loving toward all he has made" (Psalm 145:13). Describe a situation in your life when you needed to be reminded of God's promises. How does God remind you of His love?

3. How has God refined you through a difficult situation at work or at home?

*Father, help me cling to Your Word and Your precious promises.*

## Chapter Nine

# God Is My Security

*"Let the beloved of the Lord rest secure
in him"* (Deuteronomy 33:12).

### *Growing Flexibility*

I stood at the threshold of 1998. The shackles of the welfare system lay shattered at my feet. I felt like an eagle perched on the edge of its nest, waiting to soar on the air currents. *Father, thank You for Your mighty deliverance. You are totally faithful. Thanks for the future You have planned for us.*

Now I was working thirteen hours a week at ACTS. Daily life was more peaceful than it had been in months. *Father, how do You want me to spend these extra hours I have?*

"Spend more time with Me," God said quietly, "and I'll show you how to spend the rest of your time."

*Father, I want to be as close to You as possible. Help me keep You as top priority in my life. Help me guard my time alone with You.*

One day in January, eleven-year-old Jonathan asked, "Mom, can I be homeschooled now that your job has changed?" Last fall I had often thanked God that Jonathan was in public school. I couldn't have taught him then with all the chaos in my life. Now our circumstances were totally different.

I thought and prayed about Jonathan's request for several weeks. Reasons for bringing him home far outweighed any reasons for keeping him in public school.

*Father, I'm confused. Last summer You clearly revealed Your plan to send Jonathan as a missionary to the public school. What's going on now?*

"Are you willing to change course unexpectedly if that's how I lead you?" God asked.

*What would the teachers think? Or friends? Or relatives? I'd look scatterbrained and irresponsible taking him out of school mid-year.*

"You're more concerned about what others think than what I think. If I change directions, will you follow Me? Or will you insist on the old plan? Jonathan has shared My love with the students and is praying daily for his classmates. Consider it a short-term mission trip. Will you follow as I lead you now?"

*Father, forgive me. I'm slow to change directions once a course is set. I didn't realize homeschooling Jonathan was part of Your plan for us right now. I want to please You, not people. I choose Your way. I'd love to have him home again.*

Homeschooling my three children put us all on one schedule. It provided daily opportunities to understand and appreciate one another. It brought us closer together as a family. *Father, thank You for this opportunity to teach all my children at home. Please keep me flexible in Your hands, allowing You to redirect me at any time. Help me always embrace Your leading in my life.*

I registered Timothy for a homeschool biology lab class offered at a local college. Then carpooling plans fell through. *Now I'll have to drive him twenty miles each way, once a week, for the whole semester. What a waste of my time.* To my surprise, I enjoyed the time alone with Timothy in the car. We talked about his class and upcoming events. Sometimes we stopped for ice cream cones on the way home. *Thanks, Father, for this unexpected time with Timothy.*

God blessed me with another surprise: Timothy's weekly three-hour class provided uninterrupted writing time for me. I'd drop him off at his class, walk to the college library, and write in one of the study rooms. *A quiet place to think, pray, and write—what a gift, Father. You've creatively carved out time for me to write. Please keep me flexible to Your plans.*

### God's Economy

My children and I read a book together about George Mueller as part of our homeschool studies. For over sixty years, he trusted God to meet his family's needs and also provide for the thousands of orphans in his care. And God, in His perfect timing, always provided. *Father, I want to be that dependent on You. I want such stability and security in You that I cannot be shaken.* George Mueller's written account of God's faithfulness stirred something deep within me. *Father, I want to write the testimony of Your faithfulness to our family. I want our story to encourage others to fully trust You.*

George Mueller's generosity intrigued me. Even when he had little, even when he didn't know how his needs would be met, he still gave generously to others. *How could he do that, Father? Wasn't he afraid he'd give away what his family needed?*

"He trusted Me to provide for his needs," God replied. "Giving is a way to express My love to others. Giving also shows that you trust Me to care for you. Freely you have received, Linda. Freely give."

My income from ACTS plus child-support was equivalent to what we had received on welfare. Money God provided in December helped cover our current expenses. I didn't know how we'd make ends meet in the future. *Father, I want to be generous like You. I have gladly tithed my income all these years. Now I sense You want to expand my capacity to give. Help me trust You for our needs as I share what You've given us.*

I bought a book to encourage a new mom. I blessed a favorite babysitter with a letter and money. I contributed toward a young woman's mission trip expenses. *Father, thanks for filling me with Your joy as I give to others.* A few days later, I received an unexpected check in the mail. Then another family gave me fifty dollars. *Everything we have comes from You, Father. I can't out-give You, can I?*

"Enjoy all that I give You," God said, "and freely share it with others. You will never lack."

My car insurance payment was almost due. When an insurance ad came in the mail, I called for a price quote. The company offered my exact coverage for $140 less, for six months. *Thank You, Father.*

My friend Pam called. "Linda," she said, "airfares are really low right now. I'm sending $100 toward a ticket so you can come and visit me."

*Father, Your economy amazes me. The surplus from my car insurance will cover the rest of my plane ticket.*

A friend contacted an accountant to file my tax return. *Thank You, Father. I never expected such a large refund!* I relaxed about our finances while I waited for that check to arrive in the mail.

"You're trusting in a check you haven't seen," God said gently. "You're calm and peaceful because you believe it's coming soon."

*That's right, Father. It will meet many of our needs in the months ahead.*

"Linda, I own the Bank of Heaven with unlimited resources. I am much more dependable than a refund check from the government. You can live peacefully, no matter what your income, because I will provide everything you need. Trust Me completely."

### Time to Write

Many opportunities came my way during January and February: a radio interview, homeschool field trips, and more speaking engagements. I could attend a conference, teach a Bible class, and lead a family camp weekend. They all involved the use of my time. *Father, how can I know which activities to pursue and which ones to turn down? I want to honor You with my time.*

"Bring each opportunity to Me and listen for My voice," He said. "I will instruct you and teach you in the way you should go; I will counsel you and watch over you" (Psalm 32:8).

Homeschooling, working at ACTS, and Friday-morning writing sessions took much of my time. But I had many more interests, and other ministry opportunities tugged at my heart. *Father, I want Your priorities in my life. I need Your discernment. What do You want me to focus on right now?*

"This is the season to write," God said clearly.

*Father, I trust You. Your ways are always best. I'm willing to write as You lead me.* Writing became the filter I used to evaluate any possible activities. *Will this help develop my writing skills? Then I'll pursue it. If it doesn't pass that test, I won't pursue it at this time.*

In early March, I learned about an intensive three-day writing workshop. I knew that passed the test, so I submitted my application. *Father, You've given me the desire to write the story of Your faithfulness to our family. You've provided time for me to write. Now please make a way for me to participate in this workshop so I can improve my writing abilities. Only twelve people will be accepted out of the more than one hundred who apply. Please make a place for me.*

Weeks earlier, I had purchased airline tickets to fly to Pam's. God had prompted me then to ask her if I could stay a few extra days to write. *Father, You knew I would need this writing time before I did. You are so good. Thank You for the six days I'll spend with Pam. Thank You for the families who will care for my children so I can have this writing retreat.*

Two days before I flew to Pam's, my friend Bob gave me a laptop computer. "This is terrific," I exclaimed. "Now I'll complete much more writing while I'm gone. Thank you so much." *Father, Your timing is perfect.*

I loved the solitude at Pam's. I loved concentrated time alone in God's presence. One morning I read Psalm 89:1: "I will sing of the LORD's great love forever; with my mouth I will make Your faithfulness known through all generations." *Father, this is the ministry You've given me in speaking, singing, teaching, and writing. I will proclaim Your faithfulness and encourage others to totally trust You.* I spent hours writing each day. I wrote the Ram van story to submit if I was accepted for the writing workshop. I wrote the story about Jonathan's bike to enter in a writing contest. The laptop helped me complete both manuscripts. *Father, thank You for these days away with You and with Pam.*

Soon after I returned home, I received a letter of acceptance to the writing workshop. *Father, You opened up this place for me! Please use this workshop to develop my writing skills. I want You to be clearly seen through my writing.*

### Joyous Celebration

For months, my heart had overflowed with gratefulness to God. Daily I recounted specific ways God had worked in my life and family during the past years. *Father, I never envisioned all the healing and growth You would bring to my life. You just keep on loving and supporting us. We have overwhelming evidence of Your ongoing faithfulness.*

One day, God gave me the idea to have a special celebration of His faithfulness to our family. *Ten years of depending on You as a single parent family is a major milestone, Father. What an opportunity we have to honor You! It would be like a huge stone of remembrance for our family.*

When I talked it over with my children, they eagerly shared ideas of ways to celebrate and people to invite. We designed a flyer announcing our family's celebration of God's faithfulness. We sent it to many people who had touched our lives during these ten years. I included personal notes of thanks for specific ways they had demonstrated God's love to us. We invited a group of friends to celebrate with us in our home on April 4, 1998. *So many people, in large and small ways, have shown us Your love, Father. Please pour out Your abundant blessing on each one.*

Our family eagerly prepared for our celebration. Rachel cut out and hung huge colored letters on our living room wall: "God is Good!" Jonathan made special bookmarks to give our friends: "10 years—God is Good." We bought Bible verse mints to share at the party. We chose favorite songs for praising God.

I basked in God's presence on the day of our celebration. *Father, You are continually faithful. There is no one like You. Thank You for revealing Yourself to me. Father, today is completely opposite from this day ten years ago. On April 4, 1988, I desperately applied for AFDC, totally panicked about providing for my children. Today we rejoice in Your faithfulness to us throughout these ten years.*

Dear friends filled our living room, including Wes and Gretchen, Gail, and special friends of my children. Many of them had never met before, but our unity in Jesus quickly drew us together. We gave each person one of our golden stones of remembrance and encouraged them to share a story of God's faithfulness to us.

"Do you remember when we bought the camper together?" Wes began. "You practiced backing it up into our driveway for hours. We cheered you on from the kitchen window and asked God to bless you." And the camper story was told.

"Gretchen," I asked, "remember when I had my gallbladder surgery and told the receptionist at the hospital you were my 'next of kin?'" That story was shared, the Ram van story, how we started to homeschool, and many other stories. Our friends were delighted to hear how others had been channels of God's blessing to our family.

My children each played a recording of a song that had encouraged them to trust God. Lyrics revealed the truths

God had anchored in their hearts: "He cares for you like no one else," "I cast all my cares upon You," "Prayer is very important. When you pray, big things can happen."

I shared the story of Abiding Hope and the turning point it had been in my life. Then I sang the song. Our friends had never heard it before.

Abide in Me, Jesus said, and I'll abide in you
In Me there is fullness of life
Come rest in My embrace and daily seek My face
In Me alone you will find:

Abiding Hope, to guide you through the night
Abiding Hope, so in the darkness you'll see light
Abiding Hope, to keep you anchored
    through the storms
I'm here to be your Abiding Hope

He's changing me deep inside
And I'm still learning to abide
He's my joy, He's my fullness of life
My strength for each new test, my peace, my quiet rest
In Jesus alone I have found:

Abiding Hope, to guide me through the night
Abiding Hope, so in the darkness I'll see light
Abiding Hope, to keep me anchored
    through the storms
My Jesus is my Abiding Hope
My Jesus is and always will be my Abiding Hope

Peaceful silence filled the room as we pondered God's goodness. A few minutes later, Wes spoke. "Linda, that song describes what has happened in your life during these years," he said. "You've been living that song."

"During these years," Gail added, "others have watched your family and how you have responded to situations. Your life is a testimony of God's faithfulness."

"I marvel at how you take every opportunity to teach your children that God will provide," Kristen commented. "I'm excited to see how God will use them."

"My life is much richer because you've been in it," Wes affirmed. Others nodded in agreement.

*Father, ten years ago, I was isolated and cut off from others. I didn't have a handful of friends. Tonight I thank You again for the treasure You've given me in these friends.* Our living room overflowed with thanksgiving, love, and laughter. We could have sung praises to God all night long. As our friends prayed for our family, a joyful expectancy bubbled up within me.

*Thank You, Father, for all You have planned for us in the years ahead. You are launching our family into a bright new future. Please continue Your life-changing work in my heart. I trust You completely.*

### God's Tapestry

I eagerly anticipated the first day of the writing workshop, still several days away. As I reflected on our celebration of God's faithfulness, He showed me something I had never seen before. God brought to mind numerous ways He had prepared me to write about His faithfulness. "Linda, think about the writing course you took," God began. "You started it in 1988."

*That's when You provided the money for that correspondence course and the typewriter. You motivated me to get up and write at 5:00 a.m. while my children were still sleeping.*

"Remember the 1990 Christian Writer's Conference?"

God asked. "That's where I birthed in you a vision for writing a book."

*The idea completely overwhelmed me then. I remember crying out to You and how You answered: I don't know how to write.*

"I do. I'll write through you."

*I don't know the market.*

"I do. I will teach you."

*I don't have a vision.*

"I do. I will give it to you."

*I don't have the words.*

"I do. I will inspire you. 'My grace is sufficient for you, for my power is made perfect in weakness'" (2 Corinthians 12:9).

*Your encouraging words comforted my trembling heart.*

"Now think about the computers I provided for you," God encouraged. "The first arrived in 1993."

*I couldn't imagine what I'd ever need one for.*

"Then in 1994 another family gave you their computer, printer, and computer desk."

*I thanked You and asked You to help me learn how to use it.*

"Do you remember what happened in 1995?"

*I do.* Two different events ran through my mind: One afternoon at Kelli and Bob's home, Bob announced, "Linda, I've got a computer for you."

"Thanks," I replied, "but we got a computer last year from some friends."

"What kind is it?" he asked. "Does it have Windows?"

"I don't know. What are Windows?" Then I learned that Bob got old computers from work, fixed them up, and gave them to people he thought could use them. It was his way of blessing others.

"You'd really like this computer. It's very easy to use,"

Bob reassured me. He brought it over and set it up. I felt grateful for the computer but intimidated by it, too.

*Thank You, Father. Please help me learn to use it.*

A few weeks later I met Randy, who had set up the church computer system. "I'll teach you some computer basics," he offered. He gave me several lessons before he moved overseas.

*Randy helped me overcome my fear of computers. For the first time I understood how useful a computer could be for writing.*

"You and your children read a little book called *Realities* by Basilea Schlink in the spring of 1997," God reminded me. The stories were short simple excerpts from life: specific problems, prayers, and answers.

*I remember my conversation with my children after we finished the book:*

"Let's list all the ways God has answered our prayers," I encouraged.

"The two trips to Grandma and Grandpa's," Jonathan said.

"Our piano," Rachel added, "and God healing me of my headaches."

"This house," said Timothy, "and the washer and dryer."

"Our two cars."

"Our mission trip to Mexico."

"A bike just my size."

We quickly filled the page. *Father, this is the heritage You've given our family. For the first time, I can envision writing a book about Your faithfulness to us.*

"I used *Realities* to inspire you, Linda. Your vision and desire to write of My faithfulness grew strong after that."

*You're right. And I attended a book writing seminar that summer to learn how to start writing a book.*

"Ah, yes," God replied. "Remember how prayer became predominant after that seminar, after you and I had a heart-to-heart conversation?"

*Yes, Father. I cringe to think how I might have taken off with my own plans if You hadn't confronted me.* God's words and my response were etched in my mind and heart.

"You want to write this book," my heavenly Father said during the seminar, "but you haven't consistently sought My wisdom or direction. I am Your source. I planted the seed for this book in your heart years ago. Look to Me."

*Father, forgive me for putting my hope in this seminar instead of in You. I want my writing to be birthed out of intimacy with You. I will diligently seek You about every part of it and only write as You lead me. Please reveal Your plans to me.*

"Your life was filled with uncertainty and upheaval during the fall months in 1997," God said. "Through those difficult situations I revealed My love and faithfulness to you."

*Father, Your faithfulness to me during those turbulent months ignited my passion to proclaim Your faithfulness to others.*

"Remember how I provided time for you to write in 1998?" God asked.

*My smaller job, Timothy's weekly biology class, and my writing retreat at Pam's helped me focus on writing. Never before have I had such consistent, concentrated time to write.*

"Your writing instruction, computers, the vision from Me for writing, your prayers about writing, and the time I provided for writing—all these are interwoven with the happenings of your life. Together they are all part of My special design for you."

*Father, I recognized Your hand when each of these individual events occurred. But now, for the first time, I see how they are all connected and part of Your bigger plan for my life. It's like seeing a beautiful tapestry for the first time.*

"Linda, think about your recent celebration of My faithfulness to your family," God encouraged. "It proclaimed My faithfulness in your past, yet also launched you expectantly toward the future."

*Father, Your faithfulness is indelibly woven throughout the experiences of my life. Your faithfulness holds my life together!*

### True Identity

After our celebration of God's faithfulness, I realized how much I had changed during the past ten years. *Father, I'm a different person now. I used to panic about car problems. I used to cringe at every change in the welfare rules. I used to worry in the summer about having money for winter coats and boots for my children. I used to think You would get tired of caring for us. I used to think You would get sick of hearing from me and tell me to work out my own problems. I still don't like car trouble, and I still face struggles in my life, but You have changed my heart.*

*The place of greatest stability and rest is in Your arms. You designed me to always be dependent on You. You love taking care of me! You delight in hearing and answering my prayers. Your loving-kindness has drawn me into Your embrace. Now I know You intimately as my Father. I know beyond any doubt that You are with me. You will never leave me or forsake me. You are my provider and protector, my closest and dearest friend.*

During a worship service one Sunday morning, the pastors prayed individual blessings over the people. "Father," a pastor prayed for me, "may Linda know absolutely, without any doubt, that she is Your daughter. Give her great delight in learning who she is and how You've designed her."

Then he said to me, "Don't connect your identity to your position, Linda. You're not a single mom; you're a daughter."

*Father, before everything else, I am Your daughter. That's what You've taught me throughout these years. In 1988 I only saw myself as a single mom—abandoned, helpless, and hopeless—my life collapsing before my eyes. But You have revealed how You see me. I am loved, precious, and a delight to You because I am Your daughter. Thank You for these years of learning to know You as my Father and finding my security in You.*

"I love you and care for you," God reminded me, "not because of what you do, but because you are precious to Me."

*Father, I know You are always working on my behalf. You love me and care for me more than anyone else can. I will keep on trusting You and telling others of Your faithfulness.*

"My precious daughter, you bring Me great joy and delight. Rest in my love as I care for you."

*Father, You are forever faithful. Thank You for Your extravagant love and Your tender ways of caring for me as Your daughter. Your ways of providing are infinite. You have the resources of the universe at Your fingertips. You are my security. Absolutely nothing in this world can compare with living in Your presence, being wrapped in Your loving arms, and trusting You completely. You have been, You are, and always will be my Abiding Hope. As I continue on this daily journey of faith, I will proclaim Your faithfulness.*

\* \* \*

1. Where have you looked for security in the past? How does it compare to the security God freely offers you?

2. What's the difference between your role and your identity? Where does your identity come from? According to 1 John 3:1a and Romans 8:15b-16, how does God relate to you? When you embrace your identity as God's child, how does it influence your thoughts, feelings, and behavior?

3. Read Lamentations 3:22-23. How do you or could you celebrate God's faithfulness in your life?

*Father, You are my security. I embrace You and Your plans for my life.*

*Chapter Ten*

# Questions to Ponder

1. Which truth about God deeply comforts you right now?
Why?

God is my provision.   God is my refuge.

God is always with me.   God is faithful.

God is for me.   God keeps His promises.

God restores my hope.   God is my security.

God is trustworthy.

2. How has God ministered to you through this book?

3. Who do you know who needs the encouragement and
hope this book offers?

Please contact the author with your comments about
*God, I Need Help.* Send your response to:

Abiding Hope Ministries
P.O. Box 23506
Minneapolis, MN 55423-0506
www.abidinghope.com

## Chapter Eleven

# God's Promises For You

"For the eyes of the Lord move to and fro throughout the earth that He may strongly support those whose heart is completely His" (2 Chronicles 16:9, NASB).

"For I know the plans I have for you," declares the Lord, "plans to prosper you and not to harm you, plans to give you hope and a future" (Jeremiah 29:11).

"I have loved you with an everlasting love; I have drawn you with loving-kindness" (Jeremiah 31:3).

God has said, "Never will I leave you; never will I forsake you" (Hebrews 13:5).

Do not be anxious about anything, but in everything, by prayer and petition, with thanksgiving, present your requests to God. And the peace of God, which transcends all understanding, will guard your hearts and your minds in Christ Jesus. (Philippians 4:6-7).

*"For I am the* LORD, *your God, who takes hold of your right hand and says to you, Do not fear; I will help you"* (Isaiah 41:13).

*"Call upon Me in the day of trouble; I shall rescue you, and you will honor Me"* (Psalm 50:15, NASB).

*"I will instruct you and teach you in the way you should go; I will counsel you and watch over you"* (Psalm 32:8).

*"Do not fear, for I am with you; Do not anxiously look about you, for I am your God. I will strengthen you, surely I will help you, Surely I will uphold you with My righteous right hand"* (Isaiah 41:10, NASB).

*"Blessed is the man who trusts in the Lord And whose trust is the Lord. For he will be like a tree planted by the water, That extends its roots by a stream And will not fear when the heat comes; But its leaves will be green, And it will not be anxious in a year of drought Nor cease to yield fruit"* (Jeremiah 17:7-8, NASB).

*The* LORD's *lovingkindnesses indeed never cease, for His compassions never fail. They are new every morning; Great is Your faithfulness* (Lamentations 3:22-23, NASB).

## Chapter Twelve

# Our Story Continues

Six years have flown by since our celebration of God's faithfulness. I never imagined all the new opportunities God would give us to trust Him.

I continued homeschooling my children through their high school years. God provided unusual learning experiences to expand our education. The flexibility of homeschooling allowed us to embrace those opportunities. A friend of ours was walking across the nation, praying for America. We decided to drive to Iowa and spend three days walking and praying with him and his family. They invited us to stay longer and travel and pray with them. When I prayed about it, God said, "If you go with them, I'll use you." We did, and God did. We visited a church on Sunday morning and ended up leading worship! During the next seven days, we saw God provide meals and shelter, and arrange remarkable conversations. Walking and praying across half of Iowa was a once-in-a-lifetime experience.

My children pursued their individual interests while homeschooling. One year, Tim apprenticed with the owner of a home-repair business. Tim received valuable hands-on training in addition to time and conversation with a Christian man. At age fifteen, Rachel traveled to the Ukraine and served in an orphanage for ten days. She discovered for herself that when God leads you to serve Him, He also provides.

Tim graduated from Abiding Hope Academy, our homeschool, in 2000. Then he attended YWAM's Discipleship Training School in Colorado. Three months of training plus a two-month overseas outreach cost $5000. My children and I asked God to meet his needs. Tim worked, saved money, and contacted people for prayer and financial support. God provided. Tim's outreach was in Japan.

In December 2000, our Ram van died when Rachel, Jonathan, and I were in Wisconsin. It needed a new engine. Does this sound vaguely familiar? We were ninety miles from home. I didn't have money for repairs. But I knew God would take care of us. He provided a ride home. The following week a man transported the van to Wes's house. Wes helped find an engine. Then a young mechanic offered to put the engine in at no charge.

"Let's store the engine until I can pay for the labor," I told him. "Then you can put it in."

"I'll put the engine in the van this weekend," he replied. "My family had similar problems when I was growing up and peopled helped us. I just want to give back a little of what I received." And he did.

I still needed money to pay Wes for the engine. God provided an unexpected twelve-hour job helping a woman move her business. I also worked extra hours at the bookstore when my co-worker went out of town. A few days later, I found a note in my computer from fourteen-year-old Jonathan. "You can use the $500 from my 'computer fund' to help pay for the van engine." I couldn't believe it. He'd been saving his paper route money for a computer for two years.

"Jonathan," I said, "tell me about this note. What's going on?"

"I was praying about the van," he said," and I thought God said to give you my computer money. I wasn't sure if it was God or not. So I said, 'God, if you want me to do this, have someone else take care of the labor costs.' When the mechanic said he'd do the labor for free, I knew God was telling me to give you this money."

"But Jonathan, getting a computer is so important to you."

"If God wants me to have a computer," he replied, "He'll work it out. This money is for the van."

Three weeks later, a man knocked at our door and wanted to see Jonathan. "I heard what you did with your computer money," he said. "I want to bless you with this computer." He handed Jonathan a computer monitor and they set up a Gateway 2000 computer in Jonathan's room!

In March 2001, new owners of our duplex informed us of a rent increase of $500 per month. I gave my sixty days' notice to move and asked every person I knew and every group I participated in to pray for us. I searched for weeks and found only one affordable duplex. It was available a month before our lease ended. God intervened in an amazing way. The owner agreed to hold it for us if we would do all repairs on the house. With help from many friends, we replaced broken windows, repaired damaged walls, rewired old electrical wires, and cleaned and painted the entire duplex. It looked brand new when we moved in!

That summer, Tim worked as a camp counselor. One night, a tornado destroyed the entire camp while campers and staff huddled in storage rooms. That harrowing experience deepened Tim's relationship with God. A year later he went on staff with YWAM. This required a new step of faith, since he needed to raise his monthly support for the year. We asked God to provide out of His limitless resources. He did. Tim co-led two outreach teams to Kyrgyzstan that year.

On April 25, 2003, a friend told me of a single-family house available to rent at the end of May (when my lease ended). I had no thoughts of moving. We hadn't even lived in our new duplex for two years. But the more she described the house, the more interested I became. I had always wanted to live in a single-family home. And this one had a den I could use for writing!

There was one complication. May 31, the day we would have to move, was the day of Rachel's homeschool graduation. We had already reserved the church for her personal graduation ceremony. My parents had already purchased their plane tickets, and Tim had tickets to fly back from YWAM for that day. After praying about this unexpected opportunity, I talked with Rachel. I knew her initial response would clearly indicate whether to pursue moving or drop the idea. She quickly replied, "Mom, we can move in the morning and have graduation in the afternoon!"

That's exactly what we did! On May 31, God provided many people at both homes to help us. They moved all of our belongings in two hours. One observer said the workers looked like an army of ants! Then we switched gears for a fantastic graduation celebration. After the ceremony, a family hosted Rachel's graduation party in their home. Throughout the day, God reminded me of the enormous family we have in the Body of Christ.

After graduation, Rachel attended YWAM's Discipleship Training School in Colorado. God provided abundantly for all her needs. Her outreach team lived in Kenya for two months. Now she is on staff with YWAM. Raising $11,000 in support for the year has been a huge step of faith for her. We are confident God has called Rachel to this leadership position, and we believe He will provide for all her needs.

Jonathan will graduate from Abiding Hope Academy next year. He has pursued his lifelong interest in China by studying Chinese history and teaching himself to speak Mandarin Chinese. Last summer he spent a month in China, sharing God's love with Chinese teens and helping them improve their English.

In five years, my children have gone on seven mission trips to three different continents. They didn't have the money needed to go on any of them; neither did I. We have learned that money is not the deciding factor in pursuing any endeavor. Hearing God's voice and following His lead are what's most important. God provides as He leads.

My children provide endless opportunities for me to trust God. I keep releasing them to God as they serve Him worldwide. I depend on His grace and comfort when we are continents apart and unable to communicate by phone or e-mail. I remember that my children belong to God and are only entrusted to me for a short time. My days of parenting are nearly over; my days of praying for my children will never end.

In 2004, we were blessed to all live together at home for ten weeks. I treasured those days. I loved our mealtimes together. I loved singing and playing guitars together. I loved worshiping God together as a family at church. I loved talking together in the living room at night, sharing concerns or decisions to be made, and praying for one another.

We have a colorful history of God's faithfulness in our family. Each "stone of remembrance"—what God has done for us in the past—spurs us on to trust Him in the future. I delight to see my children, now twenty-two, twenty, and eighteen, radically trust God in their own lives. They hear God's voice and follow Him. How blessed I am to be the mother of my children! I see in them an uncommon depth of faith in God, a simple trust in the God who loves them and continues to provide for all their needs. Lessons we learned as a family are now being lived out in their daily lives.

> *We have run to God for safety. Now his promises should greatly encourage us to take hold of the hope that is right in front of us. This hope is like a firm and steady anchor for our souls* (Hebrews 6:18-19, CEV).

# About the Author

Linda Joyce Heaner is passionate about proclaiming God's faithfulness.

Using her gift of teaching, she creatively presents the truths of the Bible and applies them to daily life. Linda's love for God's Word is contagious. In her down-to-earth, often humorous style, she challenges and equips people to anchor their lives in Jesus Christ. She helps others recognize God's presence and celebrate His faithfulness in their lives.

Linda has an AA degree in Ministerial Training and a BS degree in Education. She is a CLASS graduate (Christian Leaders, Authors, and Speakers Seminar). For fifteen years, she has spoken at retreats, Bible studies, seminars, and inspirational programs throughout the Upper Midwest. She has led workshops at Hearts at Home regional conferences. Topics she presents include: Cultivating a Thankful Heart; Stones of Remembrance: Building Spiritual Memory in Your Family; Encourage Me!; and God Recycles.

Linda's stories have appeared in *Stories for a Teen's Heart*, Vol. 3 (Multnomah), and in magazines, including *Focus on the Family* and *Homeschooling Today*. She has written "The Servant's Praise Service," a contemporary worship service. Linda has thoroughly enjoyed home-schooling her children during the past ten years. Her family is featured in the chapter "Homeschooling Single" in *Real-Life Homeschooling* (Fireside).

"Life is unpredictable," Linda says, "but one thing is certain. Jesus is our Hope. He is trustworthy and dependable. When we're overcome by the circumstances of life, we can cling to Him. He is our Abiding Hope."

*For additional information, or to contact Linda to speak to your church or organization, please write to:*

Abiding Hope Ministries
P.O. Box 23506
Minneapolis, MN 55423-0506
or visit www.abidinghope.com.

# Order Form

To order *God, I Need Help,* please use the order form below (please print): (Quantity Discounts are available. Please inquire at the address or Web site below).

Name: _____

Address: _____

City: _____ State/Prov: _____

Zip/Postal Code: _____ Telephone: _____

_____ copies @ $12.99US/$15.99Cdn.:    $_____

Sales Tax:
(Please add 6.5% for books shipped to a Minnesota address)$_____

Shipping: ($3.95 first book + $1.00 each add. book)    $_____

I want to donate $_____ so individuals in extreme distress can receive a book.

Payment must accompany orders.

**Total amount enclosed:**      $_____

Payable by Check or Postal Money Order
(Please make checks payable to Abiding Hope Ministries)

**Send to:**      Abiding Hope Ministries
P.O. Box 23506
Minneapolis, MN 55423-0506
www.abidinghope.com